THE CULT OF THE FACT

LIAM HUDSON

THE CULT OF
THE FACT

A Psychologist's Autobiographical
Critique of his Discipline.

'... a minute contribution to the study of the only subject that
deeply and permanently concerns us – human nature and the
ways of human thought.'

Odell Shepard, *The Lore of the Unicorn*

Harper & Row, Publishers
New York, Evanston, San Francisco

LIBRARY OF CONGRESS CATALOG CARD NUMBER: 72–11872

STANDARD BOOK NUMBER: 06–136115–1

Contents

PREAMBLE 11

1. Doppelgänger 15
2. Oxford Philosophy 29
3. Cambridge 45
4. The First Fourteen Years 57
5. The Radical Objection 73
6. The Soft and the Hard 83
7. The Question of Indoctrination 93
8. False Science 111
9. No Scientist an Island 127
10. Meanings and Actions 139
11. A New Root Metaphor 157
12. The Experiential Core 173

NOTES 179

INDEX 185

Illustrations

1. Unicorn dipping its horn into water, by Leonardo da Vinci (Ashmolean Museum, Oxford) *facing page* 48

2. Maiden with Unicorn, by Leonardo da Vinci (Ashmolean Museum, Oxford) 48

3. Rainer Maria Rilke, at the time – near the end of his life – when the *Sonnets to Orpheus* were written 49

4. An Oxford Philosopher of the 1950s, J. L. Austin (Radio Times Hulton Picture Library) 64

5. A seventeenth-century dissection of the cerebral cortex 65

6. The behavioural metaphor 128

7. Francis Galton, aged 71, photographed as a criminal 129

8. *The Ecstasy of St Teresa*, by Bernini (Mansell Collection) 144

9. Venus dissected – a seventeenth-century plate 145

Acknowledgments

A number of people have read drafts of this book, helping and encouraging me with it in a variety of ways. In a work as personal as this it would be out of place to mention them by name. I would like to thank them all here, none the less; offering them as I do so the cloak of a decent anonymity.

Parts of the argument in this book have already been published in the form of two articles: 'The Choice of Hercules', *Bulletin of the British Psychological Society*, vol. 23 (1970), pp. 287–92; and 'Intelligence, Race and the Selection of Data', *Race*, vol. 12 (1971), pp. 283–92.

I am grateful to the following for permission to quote from works in which they hold the copyright: George Allen & Unwin Ltd and Barnes & Noble, Inc., for THE LORE OF THE UNICORN by Odell Shepard; Barrie & Jenkins Ltd, for THE EDUCATORS by David Black; William Collins, Sons & Co. Ltd and The Viking Press, Inc., for TOWARDS THE END OF THE MORNING by Michael Frayn, published in the United States as AGAINST ENTROPY, Copyright © 1967 by Michael Frayn; *Harvard Educational Review*, for 'How Much Can We Boost I.Q. and Scholastic Achievement?', *Harvard Educational Review*, vol. 39 (1969), pp. 1–123, Copyright © 1969 by President and Fellows of Harvard College; and The Hogarth Press Ltd, St John's College, Oxford, and W. W. Norton, Inc., for SONNETS TO ORPHEUS by Rainer Maria Rilke, translated by J. B. Leishman.

To Bernadine

Preamble

This is a book about professional psychologists and the visions they pursue. It expresses a growing dissatisfaction with the self-consciously scientific psychology in which I myself was trained – an activity that, increasingly over the last ten years, has taken on the air of a masquerade. It has been written in the hope that, somewhere behind the paraphernalia of false science and apparent objectivity, there lies the possibility of a more genuinely dispassionate study of human nature and human action.

Such a book is bound to some extent to be autobiographical; and it is bound also to concern itself not simply with the 'facts', but with the unspoken assumptions that we all use when deciding which facts are interesting, and which trivial, a bore. For while the husk, the outward appearance of psychological research, is easy enough to describe – the facts and figures, tests and statistics – there remains the question of what it signifies. And here the difficulties could scarcely be more profound. In the search for coherence, some examination of one's own intellectual history and prehistory is essential; and in the event, this means that one must reconsider the institutions which provide that history: the universities, and the task of shaping young minds that they perform. One must question not so much what university teachers think they teach, nor what students think they are learning, but the more subterranean traffic in ideals and prejudices that all powerful teaching institutions create, and that governs thereafter the intellectual lives their products lead.

In attempting this, I have set myself to transgress certain barriers that at present hem in academic discussion, and render much of it inconsequential. Each of these barriers takes the form of a distinction, persuasive but false. The first is that between Science and Art: my belief, unfashionable though this may still be, is that all arguments bearing on human life deserve to be heard within the same arena of debate. The second is between the Serious and the Frivolous: we are moving, if the tastes of the student body are any guide, from an era in which wit, like Art, has been seen as an irrelevant frill, into one – at once gloomier and more Teutonic – in which wit is outlawed as an affront to moral rectitude. The systematic, technical and cheerless are automatically preferred to the literate and humane. Although this new Calvinism satisfies simple psychic needs, I have written in defiance of it – also on the chance that the tide of piety is one that can still be turned.

Lying behind these false distinctions, and serving to unite them, is a further and more general distinction, itself false: that between Style and Content. In the entrenched sciences, it is possible to transmit the truth in prose that is as crabbed as it is evasive. But where foundations are shakier, style not merely limits what we find it natural to express; it is, in important respects, the very essence of that expression. For it is through our style, our mode of address, that we transmit all those messages that lie beyond the literal meaning of our utterance. And it is precisely on such 'meta-messages' that the focus of this book lies.

My account begins, conventionally, with the circumstances of its own conception. Also, less conventionally, with a foray into literary criticism, and into the history of a particular myth. This may seem at first sight irrelevant, a diversion. But if I have judged matters aright, this brief literary exploration heralds my main theme – Myths, Ancient and Modern – and also serves to identify the metaphorical nature of its own motive force: the spring that moves the mechanism along. My assumption is that human thought, before it is squeezed into its Sunday best, for purposes of publication, is a nebulous and intuitive affair: in place of logic there brews a stew of hunch and partial insight, half submerged. And although we accept that our minds' products must eventually be judged by the puritan rules of evidence and insight – the strait gate through which they must pass – we seem in practice to draw what inspiration we possess from a hidden stockpile of images, metaphors and echoes, ancient in origin, but fertile and still growing. This work is no exception. Its energy is drawn from a clutch of human sentiments that, over and again down the centuries, have found expression in potent, metaphoric form. What these sentiments are, and what their relation is to a putative science of human life, should with luck become clearer as the narrative progresses.

To begin with, though, the story is simple enough – in fact, it has about it the beguiling air of a fable. In it, the intrepid young psychologist is packed off by his mentors across the deserts of ignorance and superstition. In mid-journey, with rations running low and a dead-line approaching, this outrider of the rational order is set upon – or so it seems – by the agents of unreason. Bloodlessly, as on the silver screen, his assailants tumble to the ground. But the dead will not lie still. They dust themselves down, and demand to be heard. Our hero finds that parley he must, and around the camp-fire all wax philosophical.

Doppelgänger 1

The story begins in Cambridge, in the spring of 1968; my eleventh year in Cambridge, and my third in the superlative if stagey ambiance of King's College. Those early months of the year were taken up in drafting my second book, *Frames of Mind*. This turned out to be a research report of which I am still quite proud; a compendium of the work I had done since joining King's in 1965. Perhaps it was the prospect of a move from King's to Edinburgh, from Technicolor to black and white; or of a move from the relatively free-booting world of research to a more respectable-sounding, tenured post. Or perhaps the imminence of the mid-life crisis: I was rising thirty-five, the age, so psychoanalysts tell us, when we discover that we are short of time. Or perhaps, more simply, I was a little stale. Whatever the cause, the last chapter took shape not only as a summary of the eight that preceded it, but of all the research I had then done. I felt an unaccustomed need for a simple, synthesizing statement. In terms of crudest cliché, a chapter of my working life was closing, and I wanted to round it off with a flourish.

Like its predecessor *Contrary Imaginations*, *Frames of Mind* is a book about human intelligence. In a series of studies, begun in the early 1960s, I had found that the choice an individual makes of a career, the kind of thinking he finds congenial, is related to a number of other characteristics about him: his freedom of emotional expression, his respect for authority, the masculinity or feminity of his self-perception, and so on. These associations cropped up repeatedly, though in a variety of guises, and were never entirely obscured by my stock-in-trade of tests and statistics. And this, my first effort at synthesis, produced an idea which, if not revolutionary, was at least plausible:

> It may be that a single system of values embraces the individual's perceptions of academic institutions; his perception of himself; and his demonstrable behaviour. That the oppositions between authority and freedom, self-expression and self-control, and masculinity and feminity are among the basic conflicts around which an individual's mental life develops, and that they colour his responses to a wide range of logically unrelated issues. These oppositions may be 'basic', not for arbitrary statistical reasons nor for explanatory convenience, but because they represent some of the earliest developmental crises through which each individual in this particular culture passes: the impact of parental authority; the demand for self-control, first physical and later verbal; and the establishment of a satisfactory sexual identity. This possibility of a synthesis incorporating work on intellectual abilities and interests, on perception both of self and of context, and on the upbringing and developmental crises of small children seems distinctly invigorating.[1]

The suggestion that the developmental crises of early childhood shape an individual's later intellectual life is of course quite unoriginal; it is a tenet of much recent psychoanalytic thought, and has been used convincingly, for instance, by Erik Erikson. Relevant factual work has been done, too, at Harvard, for example, in the early 1960s, under the anthropologist John Whiting; in this research, the growth in young men of typically 'male' patterns of non-verbal, mathematical intelligence was found to be tied to the presence of a father in the home during the early years of his son's life. And, at the conceptual level, the use of polar concepts – like masculine and feminine – as components of the individual's mental architecture, as determinants of what he can think and do, was already a commonplace among structural anthropologists under the influence of Lévi-Strauss.

But even if not new, my synthesizing idea was new to me and to empirically minded psychologists like me, and I was glad to have it. It made sense where there was otherwise a wilderness of uninterpreted facts. It was compatible with what I was then learning about sociology and anthropology. And it might even be true.

In that last chapter of *Frames of Mind* there were also some loose-knit speculations. It had gradually dawned on me that in their more mature expressions of intelligence, men act in the light not of the brute realities of biology and the social order, but of their own perceptions. Although our genes and hormones, health and opportunities, upbringing and schooling, set limits on what we can do, their influence is filtered in each of us through systems of perceived meaning that, in detail at least, are uniquely our own. In 1968, and late in the day, I was sidling up, in other words, to the notion of human identity: the individual's perception or model of who he is and what he can do.

At the time, my dead-line was near and my energy flagging, and I felt able to do no more than point out some obvious theoretical possibilities – a pleasantly undemanding task; to offer a few quotations; and to move towards a concluding paragraph or two.

Major alterations to the text ended early in April. The rest of April and May were spent in polishing away the worst excrescences of the prose; in the drudgery of footnotes, appendices, references; and in the last thankless check through. These rites turned out to be unexpectedly trying. Largely for domestic reasons, the dead-line was fixed: June 4th. We were

B

moving to Edinburgh on June 5th. In the event, the typescript was packed off to its publishers fully eleven days early. Yet this achievement sprang not from efficiency, but from a more subtle form of desperation. For while I was polishing this last summarizing chapter it seemed that I had something quite new to say. Initially, I tried to work these new ideas into the text, but the effect was muddling. Inasmuch as I could articulate them, they served less to illuminate than to disrupt. They persisted, none the less. Through the last fortnight of revision I had in fact the odd sense of quite another book writing itself in the back half of my mind; one that commented upon, complemented, recast, even contradicted, the book I was trying to finish. In the end, this shadow became so obtrusive that I shot its more corporeal double off to Methuen with the final finicking only three-quarters done.

The next step, clearly, was to write this other book down, to see what it looked like. Unfortunately, various causes conspired to produce a delay. Some were practical: a new job, a house to set straight. More pressing, though, was the fear that this doppelgänger might turn out to be not merely high-flown, but outlandish. This fear had an obvious source. For the intrusive ideas centred not on a psychological theory, nor even on a prose-borne hunch, but on an imperfectly remembered poem. The poem, in fact, was the only part of this web that my mind could clearly grasp. The rest was more elusive, no more than a sequence of vague images and implications. The poem was Rilke's famous sonnet about the girl and the unicorn; written towards the end of his life, and part of the astounding outpouring that, within three weeks, yielded the fifty-five *Sonnets to Orpheus* and the *Duino Elegies* on which his reputation now turns. I had read the sonnet in English translation from the German as a semi-literate schoolboy, and it had stuck, one of the few snatches of verse my head contained. Here it is, in Leishman's version:

This is the creature there has never been.
They never knew it, and yet, none the less,
they loved the way it moved, its suppleness,
its neck, its very gaze, mild and serene.

Not there, because they loved it, it behaved
as though it were. They always left some space.
And in that clear unpeopled space they saved
it lightly reared its head, with scarce a trace

of not being there. They fed it, not with corn,
but only with the possibility
of being. And that was able to confer

such strength, its brow put forth a horn. One horn.
Whitely it stole up to a maid, – to *be*
within the silver mirror and in her.[2]

As a schoolboy, I had reread it several times, and memorized most of it. Thereafter, it resurfaced occasionally, sharing the ride from adolescence to adulthood with one or two scraps of Shakespearean lyric, the first two lines of Milton's sonnet 'On his blindness', odd phrases from *Lepanto* and *The Ancient Mariner*, and some of the more obviously evocative fragments of Marvell – 'time's wingèd chariot' that hurries near, and the 'nectarine and curious peach' that 'into my hands themselves do reach'. Since its last resurfacing in 1968, I have done some delving; dispassionately examining Rilke's sonnet for the first time, and pondering its relevance to my own work. The product of these deliberations is the present book.

First, the mythical beast itself: the unicorn. I shall discuss him here without apology and at some length. And I shall do so because it is precisely our tendency to mythologize, to construct elaborate systems of ideas around a core of simple values, that provides the theme on which this book hangs.

As Odell Shepard points out in his delightful book *The Lore of the Unicorn*, belief in the physical reality of the unicorn seems to have gone virtually unquestioned for over 2,000 years, from the fifth century B.C. to the eighteenth century A.D.[3] Both Aristotle and Pliny accept it; and so too, it seems, though in slightly different form, did the Chinese. As recently as the 1860s the explorer Livingstone believed in it; and as acute a mind as Francis Galton's was willing to take the arguments at least as seriously as we now take those surrounding the Loch Ness Monster. Pliny's conception of this elusive creature seems in fact to have amalgamated three animals in which zoology now has more faith: the rhinoceros, the wild ass, and the oryx. Julius Solinus, who followed Pliny (who followed Ctesias), describes the beast in these terms:

> But the cruellest is the Unicorne, a Monster that belloweth horriblie, bodyed like a horse, footed like an Eliphant, tayled like a Swyne, and headed like a Stagge. His horne sticketh out of the midds of hys forehead, of a wonderful brightness about foure foote long, so sharp, that whatsoever he pusheth at, he striketh it through easily. He is never caught alive; kylled he may be, but taken he cannot bee.[4]

In subsequent centuries, the tale was repeated and elaborated, the horn getting longer and longer with each retelling. Rabelais, for instance, adds a characteristically erectile detail of his own:

> I saw there two-and-thirty unicorns. They are a cursed sort of creature, much resembling a fine horse, unless it be that their heads are like a stag's, their feet like an elephant's, their tails like a wild boar's, and out of each of their foreheads sprouts a sharp black horn, some six or seven feet

long ... Commonly it dangles down like a turkey-cock's comb, but when a unicorn has a mind to fight or put it to any other use, what does he do but make it stand, and then it is as straight as an arrow.[5]

The unicorn found its way, too, into the Bible; for instance, into Isaiah xxxiv 7: 'And the unicorns shall come down with them, and the bullocks with the bulls; and their land shall be soaked with blood, and their dust made fat with fatness.'

From earliest times, the unicorn's horn – like the rhinoceros's – was credited with magic powers. And although it was esteemed, like most horns, as an aphrodisiac, its special qualities were held to be prophylactic. It was the best of all available safeguards against poison: by dipping its horn into water, the unicorn was thought to detect the presence of any poison and to neutralize its effect. Consequently narwhal tusks masquerading as unicorn horns were highly prized, especially among influential, poisonable statesmen and clergy of the Renaissance. Indeed, most of the more prestigious treasure-houses of Europe contained specimens.

The unicorn was also embodied in at least one of the myths assimilated to the symbolism of the pre-Reformation Church. This is the story of La Dame à la Licorne, portrayed in the Aubusson tapestries now in the Musée de Cluny, in Paris, and seen there by Rilke, who described them at length. By the time these tapestries were woven, the myth was articulated in detail. Its meaning remains obscure, even so, and its origins likewise. Shepard traces the story to that Early Christian body of fable known as *The Beast Epic*, or *Bestiary*, compiled in Alexandria during the third century A.D.:

Existing texts of the *Physiologus* vary considerably in minor details, but this is the substance of what they have to relate about the unicorn: He is a small animal, like a kid, but surprisingly fierce for his size, with one very sharp horn on his head, and no hunter is able to catch him by force. Yet there is a trick by which he is taken. Men lead a virgin to the place where he most resorts and leave her there alone. As soon as he sees this virgin he runs and lays his head in her lap. She fondles him and he falls asleep. The hunters then approach and capture him and lead him to the palace of the king.[6]

As with many more contemporary myths, the allegory is tortuous, as Shepard observes:

In its simpler versions this interpretation likens the unicorn directly to Christ: its one horn is said to signify the unity of Christ and the Father; its fierceness and defiance of the hunter are to remind us that neither Principalities nor Powers nor Thrones were able to control the Messiah against His will; its small stature is a symbol of Christ's humility and its likeness to a kid of His association with sinful men. The virgin is held to represent the Virgin Mary and the huntsman is the Holy Spirit acting through the Angel Gabriel. Taken as a whole, then, the story of the unicorn's capture typifies the Incarnation of Christ.[7]

The tone of most of these formulations is distinctly prissy. Happily, one or two of the earliest versions preserve something of what was once, presumably, a more pervasive jollity:

There is an animal called *dajja*, extremely gentle, which the hunters are unable to capture because of its great strength. It has in the middle of its brow a single horn. But observe the ruse by which the huntsmen take it. They lead forth a young virgin, pure and chaste, to whom, when the animal sees her, he approaches, throwing himself upon her. Then the girl offers him her breasts, and the animal begins to suck the breasts of the maiden and to conduct himself familiarly with her. Then the girl, while sitting quietly, reaches forth her hand and grasps the horn on the animal's brow, and at this point the huntsmen come up and take the beast and go away with him to the king. Likewise the Lord Christ has raised up for us a horn of salvation in the midst of Jerusalem, in the house of God, by the intercession of the Mother of God, a virgin pure, chaste, full of mercy, immaculate, inviolate.[8]

The connotation of this 'virgin capture' theme is unmistakably erotic; and the super-imposition of a Christian moral seems to have wrenched it away from its natural course of development. From the stock of the virgin capture stories there derives the more explicit, less attractive story of the 'holy hunt'. Here the virgin acts as bait. As before, she lures the unicorn toward her, by the 'odour of her chastity'. But the unicorn is killed instead of captured, and its blood is used to heal the king's ailing son. The virgin is identified quite explicitly with the Virgin Mary; and she entices the unicorn, her Son, to bury his head in her naked lap that he may be killed by the huntsmen, who are identified, outrageously, with the Jews, the whole scheme being engineered by the Almighty in the shape of the king. Although the tableau makes wretchedly poor morality, it enacts the Oedipal potentialities of the Virgin and Son theme with a clarity that could scarcely be excelled.

By the fifteenth century – by the time of the Cluny tapestries – the unicorn had lost much of his pristine vigour. From being a ferocious, horse-like being, it had grown anaemic, fawning, moonstruck. And this insipidity was presumably a by-product of the creature's symbolic identification both with Christ, and, more generally, with the notion of purity. For the same reason, the unicorn came to be seen as male, but as sexually inert; also, though frequently portrayed as the first among animals, he was characteristically denied a mate. It has been suggested that in opposition to his more earthly double, the rhinoceros, the unicorn was seen as embodying the ideals of courtly as opposed to carnal love. Both in heraldic devices, and also in other branches of the legend, the unicorn was frequently set in opposition to the lion. The two were envisaged as mortal enemies; and were pressed into service, for the purposes of astrological symbolism, as Moon and Sun respectively.

Through such vicissitudes, the unicorn may none the less be said to preserve certain qualities: a 'remote and solitary strangeness'; the sense of being 'wild, fleet, chaste, beneficent'. It is with these central aspects of the fantasy surrounding the unicorn that Rilke's sonnet makes play.

Rilke's original description of the Cluny tapestries was rather precious in tone:

But there still remains a banquet, to which no one is invited. Expectation plays no part. Everything is there. Everything for ever. The lion looks round almost threateningly: no one may come. As yet we have never seen her tired; is she tired? Or has she merely sat down because she is holding something heavy? A pyx, one might suppose. But she inclines her other arm towards the unicorn, and the creature fawningly rears itself and climbs and supports itself on her lap. It is a mirror she is holding. Look: she is showing the unicorn its image.[9]

But by the time he came to use the myth in his sonnet, his mood had sharpened. The elements of the story, the girl and the unicorn, are in fact well suited to his mood in the *Sonnets to Orpheus*; to his preoccupation there with a sense of timelessness and purity, and of the borderline between the imagined and the real.

Granted the theme, what propositions does this particular sonnet contain? First, the idea that a creature that does not exist, or that exists only in the imagination, becomes real. Second, that the creature makes this ontological step on the strength of people's faith in its capacity to make it. Put crudely, Rilke suggests that there is a sense in which people's expectations can endow a legendary figure with substance: that given sufficient faith, the legend lives.

Until line 11 of the sonnet, Rilke leaves vague the issue of how real 'real' is; but at that point, the doubt is at least partially resolved. People's faith is sufficient to change skeletal structure; the unicorn puts forth a horn. Admittedly we are still left to wonder whether the fabled 'independent observer' of science would stub his toe on this horn in *quite* the same sense that he might on the maid or her mirror. But this margin of doubt aside, the implication is clear: expectations have a causal influence on events. And in the light of recent work in psychology and sociology, it is an assertion with a surprisingly modern ring.

More ambiguously, the poem also carries a sexual connotation:

... And that was able to confer

such strength, its brow put forth a horn. One horn.
Whitely it stole up to a maid, – to *be*
within the silver mirror and in her.

In isolation, a sexual interpretation of these lines is slightly strained. But in the light of the unicorn's history, of the aphrodisiac properties widely attributed to horns, and of the aesthetic climate within which Rilke worked, it is the denial rather than the assertion that needs support. Much of the work produced at the turn of the century, in literary and visual arts, shows a preoccupation both with death and with a somewhat morbid eroticism; Rilke himself dwells at length, for example, on the innocence and death of pre-adolescent girls – his sister had died in childhood, and he had been brought up as a girl to take her place. And eroticism was nowhere more explicit than in the work of the man to whom Rilke was secretary, and whom he admired: the concupiscent sculptor Rodin. The themes of virgin capture and holy hunt are sexual without question: the image of a son burying his face in his naked mother's lap can only with some difficulty be seen otherwise.* And the unicorn's horn can at least arguably be seen as an analogue of the male member; Rabelais was not the only writer to treat it in such a fashion.

Thus the crux of the sonnet, the words 'to *be* within the silver mirror and in her', pose a careful ambiguity. It is both directly existential and obliquely erotic. Rilke also plays off two simple ideas against one another: purity and physical sexuality. And through the device of mirror and unicorn, he manages to do so in a way that implies a sense of uniqueness, of privileged access to a world of experience from which we would otherwise be excluded. This is not just the routine *frisson* of a sexually appealing virgin, the stock-in-trade of great religious painters from Raphael to Tiepolo, but of unique access to someone else's mind. I know of only one comparable achievement, though doubtless there are many: Bernini's sculpture of St Teresa, a work to which I shall return later on.

The success of Rilke's imagery, and after many rereadings it still seems successful, lends some support to structural theories of the relation between myths, taboos and aesthetic experience. Mary Douglas, for example, suggests that taboos serve to set apart conflicting ideas or categories of experience – like sex and

---

* Shepard suggests a connection between the virgin capture theme and an ancient hunters' fable about training female monkeys to beguile rhinoceroses and thereby capture them. Here, the sexual implication is even more robust.

purity – that would otherwise create dissonance.[10] The role of myth is to mediate such conflicting categories; to provide a symbolic form of expression in which they can co-exist. Aesthetic experience can then be seen to depend both on ambiguity and on the sense of the forbidden, of edging close to topics that are taboo. As a total account of art – of Dutch landscape painting, for example – this fails. But as an account of certain kinds of aesthetic experience, especially those implicating sex or aggression or physical horror, it is quite persuasive.

Whether accurate or not as an account of Rilke's poetic intentions, structural analysis of this sort certainly helps to explain the hold of his sonnet on my adolescent imagination. Conflicts of purity and innocence, sex and guilt, bear on male adolescents everywhere.

The relevance of Rilke's sonnet to my research is another, and more complex, matter; and I shall attempt no more at present than to establish the appropriate historical connections. For Rilke's position during the first thirty years of this century was of some significance. His poems were highly regarded, and remain so – his stature being compared with that of Goethe or Keats; and his later work is now accepted as among the finer flowerings of the German romantic tradition. He was also associated, socially and intellectually, with both Nietzsche and Freud; and, to a degree that is now hard to envisage, poets, philosophers and psychologists of that generation and persuasion thought in complementary fashion. Although Rilke's expression is intuitive and Freud's systematic, they can quite sensibly be said, as Norman Brown has claimed, to accept frames of reference that are analogous: 'Perhaps Rilke needs to be supplemented by psychoanalysis. It is certain, on the other hand, that psychoanalytical formulations seem like a scrannel pipe of wretched straw when set beside Rilke.'[11]

Yet Rilke's relevance to psychology is more pointed than

this. Although he shared the same romantic, dialectical tradition as Freud, Nietzsche and Hegel, thinking characteristically in terms of impulses or categories or forces that are sharply, and at times perhaps irreconcilably, opposed, he has another more specific claim upon us: his conception of poetic utterance as a source of insight into 'the sensuous possibility of new worlds and times'. One might expect, for this very reason, that Rilke would be of interest to just those people whose business it is to explore the potentialities of the human psyche, to wit, the professional psychologists. Yet I doubt if more than a handful of the thousands now practising psychological research would see any reason – apart from the fear of seeming philistine – to give that 'sensuous possibility' space. In what follows, I hope to illuminate – and to begin to repair – the breach that this misconception of psychology represents.

Oxford Philosophy 2

In a moment of unaccustomed clarity, Sartre once suggested that the proper function of psychology was to improve the biography of the individual. That is what I now propose to attempt: to dig a little into the intellectual training I myself received.

This began at Oxford. I arrived there from National Service, and carried with me, as we all did, a sense of mild hallucination: a store of recent experience, literally true, but, in any sober context, bizarre. The memory, for example, of marching in the pouring rain through the streets of London in the Coronation ceremony of 1953 – a few paces behind the Mounties, and caked halfway up the chest in their horses' droppings. Young men with recent memories like this are hard to surprise; but they are also docile, prey to whatever pressure an institution happens to exert upon them. My position, though, was in several respects unusually strange. Academically speaking, I was a sham. At that time, Oxford colleges still awarded scholarships to young men who in their view showed signs of promise or flair. Both formally and more subtly, such scholars were treated as an elite. I had won one of these scholarships – in Modern History – to Exeter College; but in circumstances odd enough to suggest clerical error.

At school, I had been bottom of my class for the two previous years, and had failed examinations right and left. Consequently, my success at Exeter College came as an astonishment to myself and my family; and as a moral outrage to everyone else who knew me. Memories of the crucial event, the examination itself, are slight, but I do recall the Latin Unseen. This consisted of a passage in which I recognized, or thought I recognized, only three words: *Scylla*, *Charybdis*, *littoris*. My translation, submitted in desperation, concerned a young man called *Scylla*, writing love letters, *littoris*, to his mistress *Charybdis*. The college authorities were either too polite to mention this piece of witlessness; or, just possibly, they mistook it for arrogance or eccentricity; or, as I have suggested, they may have muddled my own script with someone else's.

Whatever the cause, there was a sharp discrepancy – indeed, a yawning gulf – between my exalted academic status, bearing a long gown and the scholastic ambitions of my college, and my actual academic powers. This dissonance created scenes of acute personal embarrassment. Again, though, I was lucky. In 1954, the vogue for linguistic philosophy in Oxford was at its height, and there was never a better stamping ground for an earnest, sceptical young man unencumbered with factual information. Our teachers encouraged us to confront philosophical problems head-on, rather than through our knowledge of what previous authorities had said. As a means of educating the already over-educated, this pedagogic device is unrivalled. And it was my salvation. Under- rather than over-educated, direct confrontation was the only tactic open to me. Teachers and fellow students could only conclude that I was either original or exceptionally stupid; and as I was a scholar, then wearing long hair and unconventional clothes, I was surprisingly often given the benefit of the doubt.

By the narrowest margin, and at second attempt, I survived my first Oxford examination, the Preliminary Examination in Modern History – a disgrace to scholarship, incidentally, and in that form long since abandoned. Clinging to my scholarship, and now married, I was permitted to move from History to Philosophy and Psychology, and found myself awarded a niche on the outermost fringe of the university's undergraduate aristocracy. I have never been close to people who so successfully convinced me of my own intellectual mediocrity. It was these young men who defined the context in which my presuppositions about intellectual life were formed.

The ethos of this group, or series of groups, is now a little difficult to recapture. Most of them were ex-National Servicemen; many of them knew each other before coming to Oxford, having trained together as Russian interpreters. Most, even by the standards of the day, were naive and inexperienced in personal relations. Most were politically alert, socialists of various hues. Above all, they were serious. They accepted without question the academic standards of the university, and their aim was to succeed brilliantly in their examinations. And such success they viewed, not cynically, as a passport to privilege, but as a true reflection of their worth. Later they were to discuss, almost without embarrassment, not whether they had gained Firsts, but the precise quality of their Firsts: how many Alphas they had received, how warm the congratulations of their examiners had been.

A small incident recalls this self-conscious intellectuality quite well. I was taken, on one occasion, to New College to meet a particularly prestigious member of this undergraduate world. A tall, lugubrious boy, he had won his scholarship in Classics at the early age of sixteen, rather than at a last forlorn attempt. 'Come in,' he said, looking up from his books, 'I can give you just ten minutes.' And he did.

Nearly all these young men specialized in the arts: Greats, Modern Greats, History. And uniting them, despite their diverse social and educational backgrounds, was the voice of Oxford philosophy. Since criticized for its triviality and parochialism, the philosophy practised in Oxford in the 1950s seemed to us at the time to embody all that was incisive and sane. Its most skilled practitioners we placed at the very

pinnacle of the intellectual pyramid: Austin, Strawson, Ryle.
And there was no hint in our judgment about them of know-
ingness or deprecation. There was no talk, as there is in equiva-
lent groups today, of one eminent man being played out, of
another being a neurotic, a victim of his background, a fraud.
These remarkable men we admired, and admired in terms of
their own creation. Their minds we saw as meticulous, and
their fastidiousness as extreme.

It was said, I am not now sure with how much truth, that
there were more than eighty men and women at that time in
Oxford, earning their livings as philosophers. It was their
energy and sense of purpose that brought the processes of
thinking alive to me. They created in a haphazard way an
educational environment of a quality I have never seen rivalled;
revealing to us a world in which ideas could be pursued for
their own sake, and with formidable intellectual vigour. They
offered us the chance – priceless, and accorded only rarely –
to express in terms of our work our adolescent ideals of the
scholarly life and the disinterested pursuit of wisdom. There
was no suggestion of wading through prescribed texts, of
covering a syllabus; even if ineffectually, we were grappling
bare-handed with what we took to be life's most knotty
problems. Those years spent at the periphery of Oxford
philosophy now seem an incomparable privilege: an experience that enables one to survive the more humdrum realities
of normal university life – the paper work, the career-pushing,
the committees, the almost total lack, except among the young
and uninitiated, of respect for knowledge, or pleasure in its
pursuit.

Teaching at Oxford centred on the tutorial. Attendance at
lectures was voluntary, and I attended no more than a dozen
or so in my whole undergraduate career. In the tutorial, one
was alone in a room for an hour a week with a man of great
intellectual distinction, who bent his own mind to the improve-

ment of yours. Uneconomic, and based on material privilege, this system can none the less perform wonders with those who pass through it. Again, there is an element of luck involved: in who your tutor happens to be. And once again I was fortunate, blessed with teachers of unusual gifts and patience: William Kneale and Brian Farrell.

Perhaps because Kneale was a logician, and a little out of the main stream of philosophical fashion, and perhaps, too, because I worked on my own, Oxford philosophy seems in retrospect more complex and less modish than its critics now imply. Both Kneale and Farrell encouraged their pupils to consider some at least of the perennial problems of philosophy; and neither engaged in sterile word-play. Kneale was both scholarly and kind; the kindest teacher I encountered. Farrell was altogether more combative. Every tutorial followed the same course. Farrell initially quiescent, while I turned on for him his dangerous gas-fire. Then Farrell furiously dialectic, shredding sentences into fragments: words, commas, misplaced semicolons, all about the room. Eventually, often two hours later, Farrell once more quiescent: the moment for me to turn off the gas-fire and go in search of food.

As teachers, their resources were daunting. Farrell with his nervous zeal and precision, his wild impatience with what I thought Kant thought, rather than what I thought I thought for myself. Farrell, too, with his willingness to forgo his lunch in argument with a stubborn student. Kneale because, quite inadvertently, he gave his students a glimpse of a world that still allures: that of the scholar's calm.

Two incidents stand out, both to do with Kneale. First, unexpected praise at a college 'collection': an alarming occasion in the college hall when tutors gave reports on your progress to the Rector and a few assembled Fellows – the only occasion on which I remember receiving praise from a teacher face to face. The second incident, more pregnant by far, cropped

up just before our final examinations. Most of my contemporaries had identified their examiners well in advance; and,
expert examinees, had calculated their examiners' predilections
to a nicety. Plucking up courage, I asked Kneale at the end of a
tutorial who mine would be. Half in comfort, half in reproof,
he said that he would rather drop a class than worry about
things like that. Thrown away in embarrassment, the phrase
has lingered. To someone like myself with an intense fear of
competition, and a tendency to fail examinations, such dis-
interest has a luminous appeal.

The philosophy we imbibed from such men as Kneale and
Farrell was predominantly concerned with the analysis of language; the language, particularly, that other philosophers use
in attempting to formulate abstruse ideas – the relation of mind
to matter, the basis of morality, the nature of truth, the meaning of meaning. It had a characteristically astringent flavour,
and was in certain ways stereotypically English. The greatest
weight was placed on verbal clarity; the clarity, so one is told,
that distinguished the high-placed British civil servant of the
old school, well grounded in the Classics. Stylistically, and here
Kneale was quite atypical, the Oxford manner was aggressive:
brilliant minds in dispute over the nuance of a single word.
Even when talking about moral issues, the Oxford philosophers used trivial examples; in fact, there seemed some tacit
competition to achieve the greatest possible triviality. They
teased at the logic of moral statements, but ignored the substance of morality itself. They discussed hypothetical men on
hypothetical desert islands, never real gas chambers, real Jews.

The element of artificiality in Oxford philosophy was self-
conscious, something of a game. Its somewhat narrow rationality was likewise all-pervading. We were taught to argue in an
orderly way, to examine the paradoxes and dilemmas that
language leads us into, but were steered away from the world
of feeling; of affection and hatred, impulse and intuition. We

dealt with boundaries, and with the test case; with what one could say in principle, rather than with what one wanted to say in fact. Metaphysics, any of the various forms of philosophical speculation, were all alike taboo. In a curious sense, too, what we did lacked content. It was an activity; something one did – like swimming or playing the piano. An activity essentially concerned, moreover, with the mouth, with speech. Many of the Oxford philosophers were formidable talkers: their words tumbled with a rapidity that was at times scarcely credible, yet always seeming to fall into syntactically correct patterns. And this emphasis on grammatically correct speech, on speaking 'written' sentences, was at times so extreme as to suggest that the mouth had taken on for these men and women some especial significance. Even their tones of voice were hall-marked – what now seems an implausible combination of the booming, the staccato, and the slightly nasal.

Cumulatively, the effect was deeply inhibiting. Few published; it was said because anyone trying to write already anticipated the mocking, mock-serious dissection of his words that would ensue. As a community, these philosophers lived in fear of committing a solecism – especially one in cold print: some irretractible naivety that Professor Austin could pick apart in his lectures for all to see, gaffe upon gaffe, one blunder on another. Looking back, the context they created seems one concerned, almost to the point of obsession, with the question of intellectual control. The concern for logic, the avoidance of feeling, the ideal of clarity, the hostility to metaphysics, the assumption that confusion dissolves if examined with sufficient dispassion: all these seem to have been carried over into philosophy from the classical training that so many of the older philosophers had enjoyed – a training designed by the Victorians as a means of translating tradesmen's sons into colonial administrators and gentlemen. Also Victorian was the sense that philosophical analysis was a process of cleansing; of purging from the temple of reason all that was alien and sullying. Such colonic imagery is vividly expressed, for instance, in the first chapter of Ayer's formative work *Language, Truth and Logic*. This is entitled 'The Elimination of Metaphysics'; and it begins with the sentiment – as elegant as it is tendentious – which informed much of what I myself was taught: 'The traditional disputes of philosophers are, for the most part, as unwarranted as they are unfruitful.'[1] And in the course of his argument, Ayer eliminates not only the traditional disputes of philosophers, but also such harmless creatures as the unicorn and the centaur: 'The realistic view,' he claims, 'that such imaginary objects "have real being", even though they do not exist, has already been shown to be metaphysical, and need not be further discussed.'[2]

Although he was by then in London, Ayer's influence in Oxford during the mid-1950s was still considerable. The logical positivism that he introduced from Vienna some twenty years before was philosophy conceived by scientists, and was based on the assumption that all utterances are either true by definition, as in logic or mathematics; or that they are matters of fact; or that they amount – in Anthony Quinton's excellent phrase – to mere 'noise or exhaust'. Philosophically speaking, in other words, ideas did not count, unless they corresponded directly to material objects; a view that now seems less than profound – and also self-stultifying, for *Language, Truth and Logic* is itself nothing if not a work of metaphysics.

It is possible, in retrospect, to distinguish various currents within the main Oxford stream; to distinguish, for example, Ayer's positivism from Austin's preoccupation with everyday language; and both of these from the brand of philosophical behaviourism put across by Ryle in *The Concept of Mind*. The stylistic similarity of such men was overwhelming, none the less; and I can recall, in fact, only one apparent exception to the otherwise consistently sceptical, analytic, reductive pattern.

It is a telling one, even so: we were taught very little history. Gestures were made in this direction, but my own scant knowledge of the history of Western philosophy was culled from Bertrand Russell's book of that name, informally banned in Oxford at the time. And a friend of mine could emerge from his final examinations with the highest honours, still believing that, historically speaking, Leibniz preceded Descartes rather than followed him. We found, in practice, that knowledge of Aquinas or Hobbes, Plato or Aristotle, was usable only if fed directly into more contemporary argument. We could refer to Wittgenstein, Tarski, or Carnap, but even these modest gestures were not much prized. And what knowledge we could scrounge of current fashions on the Continent – the work of Sartre and Merleau-Ponty – was of no use at all. An odd result was that eager students like myself could emerge from what was probably the best philosophy course in the world with little sustained reading behind them. I read articles, and skipped to and fro in longer works, but in two years read not a single book of philosophy from cover to cover. Our tutors assumed, I think, that we were reading as conscientiously as they had done; in fact, I sat at my portable typewriter and wrestled with my mind's nebulous contents, visiting the library only from time to time.

Despite its subtlety, its energy and its elan, Oxford philosophy seems in retrospect to have suffered a central intellectual confusion: one about the nature of meaning. Time and again, almost ritualistically, we would ask, 'But what is it to say … ?' We heard the phrase so often, repeated it so often, that it became our trade-mark. It signalled the dismemberment of a particularly juicy phrase: and we would destroy, not only for the fun of it, but in search of that phrase's core of sense. In brief, we were doing semantics. And we operated on the twin assumptions that some clear meaning could eventually be wrung from the woolliest phrase, and that only clearly definable meanings were worth the wringing. To help us we had the Wittgensteinian catch-phrase: 'The meaning is the use.' To discover the meaning of a word, you examined how people used it. But in the event, to examine the use of words is to plunge into muddle, innuendo, ambiguity, fantasy and internal contradiction. It is to discover words used for private ends, as counters in personal relations, and defined allusively, in the light of the participants' experience. To examine the use of words is to tackle the whole of psychology, sociology, cultural anthropology and semantics combined; areas of endeavour for which the Oxford philosopher was academically and temperamentally unprepared.

An oversight of such magnitude is now a little hard to credit; and my own view is in all probability an oversimplification of what was happening in Oxford at that time. Stuart Hampshire, for example, has written recently of philosophers who, like himself, turn to philosophy not as an approximation to logic or mathematics, but – quite the reverse – as an 'escape from literalness'; for whom strict argument is interesting only inasmuch as it represents the working out of an 'imaginative vision'. 'Commonsense', he says, 'and ordinary language are not the least of the confinements in which one is brought up.'[3] True enough: yet nothing so adventurous, so confidently metaphysical, filtered down to us as undergraduates, from Hampshire or anyone else. Our perception of matters, in other words, was probably a paraphrase, a caricature, of what our elders and betters thought. Yet beyond serious question, a vein of excessive rationality has run through English empirical philosophy in the last half-century. Both Russell and Wittgenstein tended to treat problems of knowledge and meaning as though they were matters of logic. And the positivists, too, had assumed that what could not be subsumed to mathematics and science could safely be ignored.

As a student, I was certainly left with the belief that all

knowledge consisted of *facts*: hard little nuggets of reality that one could assemble like building blocks into patterns. It was these patterns that constituted knowledge. This 'building block' view, in which all elements are inert and equal, is called, I have since learned, 'atomistic'; and the English tradition of thought that stretches back to Locke and beyond seems largely to have been atomistic in this sense. Whatever its virtues, the atomistic habit of mind is ill adapted to the elusive, shifting world of everyday meanings.*

Our preoccupation with evidence, similarly, made us unnecessarily clumsy. In any argument, it was on to 'the facts', the evidence, that we homed. The impulse was healthy, in that it short-circuited discussion of woolly generalities. But it was also philistine, in that an appeal to the evidence can easily deteriorate from an attempt at dispassion – a noble venture – into a verbal destructiveness that is both cheap and facile. Only more recently have I realized that the appeal to 'the facts' can also herald an altogether less wholesome enterprise: that of rendering 'scientific' or legitimate a view that is at heart ideological. But more of that anon.

Despite the strength of its hold on us, Oxford philosophy thus specified its own limitations. Theoretically, and sometimes in practice, we were driven from the plush heartland of Oxford, where the philosophers held sway, out up the Banbury Road to a seedy villa then housing the Institute of Experimental Psychology. Yet however correct philosophically, this move was as disappointing in intellectual terms as it was architecturally. For psychology in Oxford was strictly scientific in tone. Issues of perceived meaning played no part in the curriculum that faced us.

Experimental psychology in Oxford had at that time much

---

* Whether these nuggets were 'sense data' in the mind, or were objects 'out there' in the 'real world', I was never quite clear. What now seems important is that I had learnt at Oxford to think of the mind's contents as though they were physical objects.

in common with analytic philosophy; and one or two of the lecturers in the Institute had themselves read philosophy, in some cases with distinction. Others, although trained in physical or biological science, brought with them assumptions about the limits of useful knowledge which the Oxford philosophers found congenial. For psychology was defined in the Oxford Institute as the science of behaviour; explicitly, in Professor Humphrey's introductory lectures, and implicitly in every word that denizens of the Institute breathed.

Any explanation we offered, any theory we postulated, any result we described had to be defined operationally – in terms of input and output, stimulus and response. We were set to do science in exactly the way that the chemist or physicist does it. Our experiments, like theirs, had to be work that any technically competent stranger could replicate. We were practising, in Medawar's well-worn phrase, the art of the soluble. Like philosophers' examples, the experiments we performed in that little building, a converted school, had about them an air – sometimes arch, sometimes defiant – of contrivance and triviality. In dusty rooms, scruffy as only experimental psychologists can make them, we sorted cards, watched flashing lights, pressed bars, and once or twice watched white rats wander disconsolately through poorly constructed mazes. We discovered nothing of much interest, either about the rats or about ourselves; and it was never hinted that we might. Our highest ambition was to refute a theory; or, failing that, to lend it conditional support. Any idea that we were there to uncover the mysteries of the human mind, to plumb the depths of the psyche, would have been greeted with embarrassment; the kind of embarrassment that hardens into derision, and eventually into contempt. Just as a man on a desert island was held to illuminate the moral order, so a rat or monkey or student pressing a bar was thought to illuminate the brain. However odd, even mildly bizarre, such an assumption can now be made to seem, it unquestionably exerted a powerful grip. And it did so for a reason that is essentially aesthetic. The belief that the truth can be laid bare by parsimonious means is inherently handsome. The conceit that this can be done by means that are trivial is perhaps inbred and even a little decadent, but attractive none the less.

Such assumptions about research were rarely discussed, and as far as I can recall, never critically examined. Sustaining them, inarticulate, were certain more pervasive beliefs about knowledge itself. Here the influences of philosophy and psychology flowed together. The attitudes to knowledge I had assimilated were a caricature of the posture of the Anglo-Saxon empiricist: the atomistic belief I have already mentioned – that science is built by piling one fact upon another; a quasi-religious faith in the ideas of stimulus and response; a distrust of any but precise, small-scale theories; a contempt for social science, and disregard for any social or cultural process; an avoidance in research of personal feelings, or personal experience; and a taste for mechanical and electronic metaphor. Above all, we believed in 'objectivity'.

To an even greater extent than the philosophers who taught us, our friendly, formidable lecturers in psychology were – in Goffman's phrase – the managers of our reality. And they were powerful precisely because they were free to control our definition of what was worth discussing and what was not. Our subject-matter was almost entirely American (likewise our textbooks, Woodworth and Schlosberg, and Osgood); learning in rats, information theory, and work on vision in human beings provided its core. We also learnt a little social psychology, and some physiology from Morgan and Stellar's handbook; material about brains and nervous systems that in comparison to the rest seemed reassuringly substantial. Most of the material we learnt is now outmoded. Its range was in any case narrow, at times eccentrically so. But what we did, we did thoroughly. And in being thorough, we acquired a crucial academic advantage: confidence in taking a piece of research apart, irrespective of the eminence its author enjoyed. In tutorials, for example, with Tony Deutsch, I learnt all there is to know about Osgood and Heyer's model of the figural after-effect: precisely wherein lay its logical, self-contradictory flaw. And the fact that Osgood had written one of our two basic textbooks afforded him no protection. (What I did not learn was to examine the significance of this new-found knowledge; to question whether it was worth knowing that Osgood was wrong.)

My introduction to Osgood and Heyer's theory displays, in fact, the strengths and weaknesses of the Oxford method well. Deutsch packed me off one week with the reference to Osgood and Heyer's article; the information that there was something wrong with it; and seven days in which to discover what. Five days passed without illumination, and the prospect of being thought stupid loomed intolerably. So I succumbed, and asked someone in the year above what the flaw was. A penny dropped that would not otherwise have dropped, and the weekly essay was written. After listening to a monotonic rendering of my essay for three or four minutes, Deutsch realized that I had got the point. We then broke off, and spent the rest of the hour disagreeing, as we had the four previous weeks, over our government's intervention in Suez – he in favour, I opposed. I had learnt a number of lessons. How closely you must read; closer by far than the authors had written. How fallible authorities can be, and how blindly their work is taken on trust by editors and colleagues. Also, though, I had learnt to believe that the figural after-effect, a strange quirk of the human eye's function, mattered more than it did.

As a group, we accepted without question our teachers' right not only to define what we should learn, but also to judge us once we had learnt it. And to judge us totally. If they judged us second-rate, as they usually did, second-rate we thought we were, and second-rate we tended to become. Willing enough to argue an interpretation in detail – about what exactly it was that followed from Ayer's view of knowledge, or the *Gestalt* theory of perception – we accepted, lock and stock, our teachers' prejudices about the limits of useful inquiry. Unwittingly, in fact, we guyed them. I am sure I was not alone, for instance, in writing essays, vigorous but barren, that destroyed the whole fabric of psychoanalytic thought on the grounds that its assumptions could not be experimentally defined.

Quite possibly, our docility in such matters was especially marked. Many months after reaching Oxford, I still swallowed with difficulty the impulse to call all figures in authority 'Sir' – even the first-year research student, Boy Scout badge in his button-hole, who gave us extra tuition in Latin. It is just possible, too, that both philosophy and psychology at Oxford were then passing through a particularly dogmatic phase; and that those who exercised academic authority over us did so with unusual self-confidence and conviction. My suspicion, though, is that every generation of students is susceptible to its teachers' presuppositions, and that these presuppositions are potent just to the extent that they are unspoken. It is assumptions, prejudices and implicit metaphors that are the true burden of what passes between teacher and taught. Facts, skills, details are in comparison ephemeral, in the sciences especially, but in the arts as well. They are also identifiable – and rejectable. What the teacher spells out, the pupil can question. What he assumes, especially from a position of unchallenged legitimacy, his pupils will tend to swallow whole and unawares.

Cambridge

3

At Oxford, psychology occupied only a small part of my interest. Had I been good enough at it, I would have done research in philosophy. Even then, though, it was clear that to contribute to philosophy in an original way, one had to be better at philosophy than almost all the professional philosophers. It was, and remains, a field in which progress is hard-won. Psychology seemed in contrast wide open: a frontier rather than a close-knit urban growth. My degree class – rather a good Second, and rather better than I expected or deserved – won me a research grant. And as I was still intent on proving to myself that I was not a dunce, it was over to Cambridge that I made my way.

Their magnificent picture-postcard scenery apart, Oxford and Cambridge are often taken to mirror one another. Adjustments in moving from one charmed circle to another are expected to be small, even imperceptible. In the case of the two psychology departments, this was so. The Cambridge Laboratory was at the time, and probably remains, the most influential in the country; the Oxford Institute was smaller, and had had a shorter life. But they shared distinctive qualities that set them a little apart from psychology departments elsewhere. They shared even their *mise en scène*: a sense of dust settling on old apparatus, of clever men – and the occasional woman – sitting at work in hideously misshapen rooms. And luck again was on my side. I moved over to Cambridge at the same time as David Armstrong, a contemporary who had read Politics, Philosophy and Economics, whose First positively irradiated excellence, and who was to become a close friend. As foreigners, we probably looked more alike than we were. Our new professor was Oliver Zangwill; a scholarly, preoccupied, subtle, and at times startlingly insightful, person, who was to suffer me patiently and at great length, and to whom I am indebted in a dozen ways. For some reason, he seemed to have the two of us confused. Certainly, he called me 'Armstrong' for most of our first two terms in Cambridge; and I suspect that it was some time before he established in his mind to which of the two scruffy presences that glowing First belonged.

I was given a desk in an annexe, a Nissen hut a mile or so from the Laboratory itself, close to the railway station. I could rarely bring myself to sit at it, and as a consequence worked almost entirely at home. The habit has lasted, but behind it is a vague sense of impropriety, and a recurring, guilt-ridden dream about a room in a college or department, full of alien furnishings, that I ought to use but neglect. A more substantial side-effect of working at home – usually in bed, as a way of keeping warm – was that I was less absorbed than most of my contemporaries in Laboratory life, and more open to the atmosphere of the university as a whole.

This tendency was reinforced by initial contacts with my new college, Emmanuel – at every turn disastrous. I was summoned to appear before, first, the Senior Tutor, and then the Dean. The Senior Tutor, a medieval historian, told me that whether I and my wife liked it or not, I would dine in college at least three times a week in term. And the Dean, a rising young churchman, after a few preliminaries on the topic of rowing, asked where I 'stood with God'. As I had no intention of dining in college, and had no religious affiliation, the outlook was bleak. Some while thereafter, attending a special dinner for the college's research students, I was placed next to the Master, another historian, now dead. He asked me what my work was. On hearing that I was interested in intelligence tests, he replied: 'Huh. Devices invented by the Jews for the advancement of Jews.' Offered, I now realize, as a provocation, the remark blighted my relation with Emmanuel College; and it was some years before I could bring myself – despite its strategic position at the top of Downing Street – even to use its lavatory.

During the eleven years I spent in Cambridge, the chief influences on my perception of academic life were the few people I met socially. And without being for a long while aware of it, this influence centred on a single institution, King's College: a citadel of the more flamboyant among the humane virtues; a place where, until quite recently (as Conant, the President of Harvard is said to have remarked), the natural sciences were 'denounced from the chair'.

Perhaps because Cambridge lacked a large school of philosophy, or because of the links between Oxford and political life in London, or because I had moved unwittingly from one kind of group or clique to another, Cambridge, compared with Oxford, seemed the less serious place of the two. The Arts Theatre and the Footlights Revue seemed nearer the centre of Cambridge students' ambitions than had anything to do with the stage in Oxford. New Cambridge friends took seriously not the role of the intellectual, but the prospect of success in journalism, films, television, novel-writing – or, simply, in conventional academic life. Such self-conscious seriousness as I found there focused on literary rather than political matters. For this was the age of Dr Leavis, and his followers browbeat one, an uncongenial experience, not for lack of intelligence, but for defects of moral sensitivity.

At Cambridge I met for the first time, too, creatures I had thought as mythical as the unicorn, as dead as the dodo: England's golden youth. At Oxford, there was social snobbery to be sure; but this impinged relatively little on intellectual life, and is associated in my memory, probably misleadingly, on the one hand with the sport of beagling, and on the other with an explicit, dandified form of homosexuality. The influence of Evelyn Waugh was apparent; and the fantasies of Oxford life that he had uttered so eloquently in *Brideshead Revisited* were being acted out there by young men scrambling up the social ladder in his wake. Yet, at Oxford, the centrally placed undergraduates had seemed to come in all shapes and sizes, and for the most part had no obvious social pretensions. From the onlooker's point of view at least, provenance did not seem to signify. In Cambridge, this was not so. Well-placed individuals were 'smart' in a strictly social sense: young men formidable in social presence as well as in examination results; theatrical in their repartee, and proud of their influence over the minds and bodies of the well-endowed young women around them. They were a group among whom, at least in the hearing of acquaintances like myself, self-consciously serious discussion never occurred.

This group exuded an air of personal excellence, drawing, as I later realized, on the Bloomsbury tradition that had been so strong in Cambridge between the two World Wars, and that had formed around the person of the novelist E. M. Forster. Its institutional basis was the small and secret debating society, the Apostles, that used to meet in Forster's rooms in King's.

The influence of King's ran directly counter to that of the scientific community, to which I was peripherally attached. And, manifestly, the tension between these two systems of value, the humane and the scientific, has informed all the work I have done since. It was the proximity of King's, I now realize, that made it easy to work outside prevailing psychological fashions. King's, therefore, deserves a brief portrayal – a tricky undertaking; and one of its more important social mechanisms, its connection with the Apostles, must be made more nearly plain. For though secret, it is the Apostles and the fantasies surrounding them that have helped to perpetuate the

1. Unicorn dipping its horn into water, by Leonardo da Vinci

Maiden with Unicorn, by
onardo da Vinci

3. Rainer Maria Rilke, at the time – near the end of his life – when the *Sonnets to Orpheus* were written

aristocratic tenor of Cambridge humanism: the sense of circles within circles, of charismatic inner groups from which ordinary mortals – and all women – are excluded. And it is just this aristocracy of tone that has thrown Leavis's nonconformist zeal into such marked relief.

In his autobiography, Bertrand Russell tells us that this group was established fully 150 years ago, and has numbered among its members 'most of the people of any intellectual eminence who have been at Cambridge since then', himself included. In his day, G. E. Moore, Keynes, Whitehead, the Trevelyans, McTaggart and Lytton Strachey all belonged. Wittgenstein, on the other hand, declined to take part. Putting together Russell's description of the Apostles with a few casual gleanings, one can detect a constant element in their deliberations; and around this, decade by decade, some more peripheral changes of mood. The preoccupation of the Apostles with their own excellence has not wavered. But the context within which such excellence is judged has been subject to substantial historical shifts. The Victorians Russell describes as relatively earthbound, envisaging themselves as future 'leaders of the multitude'. The Edwardians who followed, Lytton Strachey and Maynard Keynes, for instance, 'aimed rather at a life of retirement among fine shades and nice feelings, and conceived of the good as consisting in the passionate mutual admirations of a clique of the elite'. Where the Victorians were stoutly heterosexual, homosexual relations between Edwardian Apostles were, Russell tells us, common.

Like the influence of Waugh in Oxford, that of Strachey in Cambridge lingered on well into my time there, even though self-conscious sexual ambiguity had become more the preserve of our seniors, and the sense of timelessness that their private incomes afforded the Edwardians had begun to evaporate. More recently still, the composition of the Apostles has changed again, becoming more political; and at least one of the

D

university's best publicized and most extreme young radicals now belongs.*

There is no incompatibility, in Cambridge, between Marxist rigour and the cult of personal excellence. It is hard to believe, even so, that such psychic luxury does not eventually sap revolutionary morale. For such bodies as King's possess astonishing powers of assimilation: they take the talented but insecure, and turn them effortlessly into scholars and gentlemen. As a newcomer, you boggle at the transformation; yet, unwittingly, you are already subject to it. Clever boys from ordinary suburban homes – even, more recently, rough young lads from the Commonwealth – are taken up and metamorphosed. Within a few years, they are virtually indistinguishable from the college's Old Etonians. And despite tokens of loyalty to their roots, all combine to live the life of lettered gentility.

This is achieved, in King's at least, at the cost of a certain theatricality. It is hard, at times, to recall that the pictures are real, the port is real, that the candles in the candlesticks are real candles and not electric lights pretending to be candles; above all, that the people are creatures of flesh and bone. In my two years there as a Fellow, I found that a sense of illusion was rapidly becoming my standard experiential mode. The air of charade was all-pervasive: the sons of suburbia like myself parodied the lettered gentry; and the lettered gentry parodied the sons of suburbia parodying themselves. The little tokens of residual loyalty – the open-necked shirt, the sandals, the harsh vowel sounds – even these were parodied. Brilliant young scientists who knew nothing of life or art gave ham performances of the role: 'brilliant young scientist who knows

* The Apostles – like all secrets, as Goffman has pointed out – are surrounded by non-reciprocal relationships with outsiders, those who are not 'saved'. Such non-reciprocal relations impart a sense of importance to those in the know; and, arguably at least, they exist for no other reason. Once, soon after reaching Cambridge, I was invited by a friend to join a 'small private debating society'. Out of my depth, I found the best excuse I could, and declined. It was only years later, and by accident, that I discovered that this society and the Apostles were one and the same.

nothing of life or art'. Vain art historians gave virtuoso per-formances of art historians being distastefully vain. And the institution itself, a haven of radical enlightenment, rose re-peatedly to heights of dramatic absurdity. To the moment in a Council meeting, for example, when a stalwart of the college – his eyes a-glisten with emotion – rose to speak for the retention of college feasts: not because they were enjoyable, far from it; nor because they were traditional; but because it was our duty to the college servants to persevere.*

This is itself, of course, a gross and ungrateful parody. Re-cruitment was not divided between suburbanites and Old Etonians; nor was everyone poised at stage centre. There were dozens who worked hard and remained inconspicuous – to be cast by their peers into the role of people who were 'absolutely first class' in their subject. And as Forster himself has said in *The Longest Journey*: 'The college, though small, was civilised, and proud of its civilisation. It was not sufficient glory to be a Blue there, nor an additional glory to get drunk.' Yet, in practice, King's seems to have served less as a forcing-house in intellectual matters; more as a meeting-place for sensibilities that are genuine but alas – like Forster's – elusive. And the ethos of the college, for all its respect for intellectual achieve-ment, serves to cushion the disappointment of vaulting ambi-tion not fully achieved. Consider, for example, these rather sad passages from the college's recent memoir of Sir John Sheppard, son of a woolbroker's clerk, who grew up, a strict Baptist, in the lower- middle-class London suburbs of Peckham and Balham; and who, though he became Provost, failed to fulfil what he had earlier promised:

But he often travelled elsewhere, on Hellenic cruises or to fashionable resorts. Generally he took with him one or two

---

* Needless to say, in the face of such bravura the move to abandon feasts was aban-doned without further ado.

young men, paying everything for them, teasing them by deflating their enthusiasm for the scenery, educating them by his courtesy to everyone and his un-English way of immediately establishing human relations, in particular with hotel staff, taxi-drivers, etcetera. His French accent was Churchillian, but it served. If he met a young man anywhere who particularly interested him, he would suggest that he came to King's for the Long Vacation period of residence; and when one did so, it was nearly always agreed that he had picked a winner.[1]

Or again:

At his instigation King's invited the King, the Queen and Princess Margaret to visit the College on 27 April 1951 for a luncheon and a service to celebrate the restoration of the Chapel windows, stowed away during the War, and the completion of the interior cleaning. He scrutinised the arrangements with meticulous care: in the seventeenth draft he amended 'the Back Lawn' to 'the Great Lawn'. He probably felt this occasion to be the apogee of his career.[2]

Or this, of another of the college's knights, Sir Frank Adcock: once a clever boy from Wyggeston Grammar School in the Midlands, who was good at the Classics, and went to Cambridge rather than into a 'family pork pie business':

From time to time they [the undergraduates] might be invited to a 'black tie' dinner. His gyp, Langley, would serve the dishes and wine like the perfect 'gentleman's gentleman'. Sitting back comfortably afterwards the host, in black velvet smoking-jacket and cigar in hand, would quote, with relish of their verbal virtuosity, passages from

'Saki' or P. G. Wodehouse. Wretches who had to come up
for a gruelling week at the end of the Christmas Vacation
to take the University Scholarship Examination would
forget their troubles when swept off by him to the panto-
mime at the New Theatre.[3]

Massive social changes have occurred since Sheppard and
Adcock were absorbed by King's; and academic life itself has
become altogether more businesslike. Yet the effect of these
changes, within King's at least, seems to have been paradoxical
– heightening the sense of role-playing rather than breaking it
down. Many of the younger Fellows there in my time seemed
peripheral – as I certainly was – to the whole enterprise; im-
postors passing for the real thing. At any moment, one felt,
the joke might be over: the Fairy Godmother would snap her
fingers, and we would all troop back to those lowly stations
where we naturally belonged. Like Anthony Powell's appalling
character Kenneth Widmerpool, we had done better for ourselves than seemed right or reasonable; unlike Widmerpool,
we had nothing more solid at our backs than the anomie of
British suburban life in the years after the war.

However, little of this curiously social quality of Cambridge
humanism penetrated life in the Psychological Laboratory. Few
of its postgraduate members aspired to be gentlemen. Yet a
rival system of snobbery they did express, the nether of the two
millstones with which I was ground: the snobbery of science.
I mention it, because it acted then, and has acted since, as a
potent constraint.

Among British scientists, and with few exceptions, the pure
look down on the applied, the physical on the biological. And
all combine to look down on the social, or 'Mickey Mouse'
scientists, who are scarcely scientists at all. The ideal is to work
with one's head, not one's hands; to be conceptually neat
rather than messy. And, as elsewhere, exceptions to these rules

are usually associated with large sums of money and with popular acclaim.

Psychology stands low in this pecking order, and contains a pecking order within it. Again, the pure look down on the applied, and the clean on the messy. The experimental, usually physical or biological in background, look down on the social, industrial, clinical and educational. The psychologist of high status works in a laboratory, and studies either a sub-human species – rat, pigeon, monkey – or some simple aspect of human skill. The psychologist of low status works with human beings in their natural habitat, and studies them in their full complexity. The psychologist of high status works on problems that to the untutored eye seem trivial; the one of low status, on problems that laymen are more likely to understand.

As in all systems of social snobbery, participants are under continual pressure to appear, indeed to become, what they are not. Research problems tend as a consequence, in psychology at least, to be tackled in a manner which is more artificial than either common sense or logic would dictate. Each problem is 'promoted' until it reaches its own level of methodological inappropriateness. The social psychologist, a creature of low status, acquires higher status by being an experimental social psychologist, and working in a laboratory fitted out with booths and one-way screens. And he can achieve higher status still, in the eyes of his colleagues if not of the academic community at large, by abandoning the study of man altogether, and joining the packed ranks of the methodologists. He then criticizes ineptitudes in experiments conducted by others. He speculates, like the country divine, on how good work might be done, but never risks the doing for himself.

Among those psychologists who work with children, the situation is complicated further by the spectre of the schoolteacher. To work in schools is to risk being confused by your colleagues with the person who teaches in one. It can scarcely be coincidental that psychologists who have measured children's intelligence have armoured themselves to a greater extent than any other with the protective magic of number. Nor can it be coincidental that in the course of half a century, the mental testing movement has told us little about children that we did not already know, but has made major contributions in the field of statistics. On the Continent, such rituals take a different outward form, but their essentials are the same. Piaget, for example, has encased his brilliant studies of problem-solving in small children in a system of logico-mathematical symbolism that few if any of his admirers read, that has no detectable explanatory point, and that only logicians can disentangle.

As Gombrich has implied, science, like art, is born of itself, not nature. Psychology is no exception. It is by reading the literature, by listening to gossip over tea in the department, by an intuitive grasp of his supervisor's prejudices, that the tyro fixes on an experiment to perform. And in psychology, a subject where mastery is weak, this cultural process can be seen with a special clarity. For where discovery in physics, chemistry or molecular biology is cumulative, psychology proceeds more by fits and starts; a series of lunges into the surrounding darkness. It is a subject, or series of subjects, in which one research fashion succeeds another, leaving surprisingly little behind it as a residue of re-usable knowledge. In this respect, even the most experimental forms of psychology resemble much more closely an art form, modern painting for instance, than they do an established science.

In such a situation, prejudices are potent. And they are particularly so, in science as elsewhere, for being implicit. The tough look down on the tender, but unless hard-pressed, deny that they do so. If cornered, they point to the unfortunate fact that, among psychologists, it is the weaker students who specialize in the more humane branches: those with lower seconds, young ladies with an interest in people. It follows, the tough point out with evident regret, that standards are lower in the more humane fields. The argument is a tricky one to combat, especially as its prophecies are self-fulfilling. As teachers and examiners, the tough-minded are in a position to give their own assumptions weight. With minds as open as any can be, they design courses and set papers that favour candidates whose style of intelligence suits them to experimental research. They thus operate a self-perpetuating social system. And being men of good faith and sociological naivety, they are free to deny that they do so. The more tender-minded know that a form of snobbery is being exercised at their expense, yet cannot convince themselves that it is groundless. They feel not merely embarrassed, but embarrassed about feeling embarrassed. And there are few more potent mechanisms for ensuring that a particular type of research is not done; or, if it is done, that it is not done well.

The First Fourteen Years   4

Almost all the research I have done since moving to Cambridge in 1957 has had a focal centre in the notion of intelligence; or, more strictly, in its determinants – those aspects of an individual's personality and circumstance that lead him to think in one way rather than another. And on the face of it, this work has had no connection with unicorns at all. In terms of style or stance, it has been remote from the intellectual tradition Rilke's sonnet represents. There are links, none the less; and the more I have looked, the more I have found. Some – the more accessible, but less interesting – are thematic, in the sense that, despite appearances, research and sonnet have subject-matter in common. Others, more subtle, bear on the philosophies, or views of knowledge, or frames of mind, or *Weltanschauungen*, that research and sonnet suggest. Touching here and there on the first, I shall concentrate on the second. And if philosophies of life or research sound a woolly or falsely grandiose topic, I can only say that from my own point of view, that of someone who tries to do research, it is down-to-earth in the extreme.

My concern with intelligence had an identifiable if inauspicious source: in a knock on the head I received, or thought I received, whilst playing rugby in the army during my National Service. This knock resulted in loss of memory and persistent headaches; and the latter I carried with me to Oxford. On failing my first examination there I was put through the screening procedures devised by the local mental hospital for the university's mentally disturbed students. My intelligence was tested. I completed the Thematic Apperception Test and

57

the Minnesota Multiphasic Personality Inventory, and my physique was measured in various ways. Gradually, the headaches disappeared of their own accord; I passed my examination at second attempt; and was left with an odd item of information about myself: that I possessed a bias of intelligence in marked degree. Tactfully, the psychologist at the Warneford Hospital told me that my facility with words was 'rather below average' for an Oxford undergraduate; but that I was good with shapes and patterns. Such a bias is just what I would nowadays expect to find in a student moving, as I then was, from Modern History towards Psychology. But at the time it seemed no more than a personal quirk or idiosyncrasy, like being lefthanded, or lacking sinus cavities, or being without the normal number of layers of skin. And when the time came to choose a subject for postgraduate research, I could think of nothing better to study than biases of intelligence. My research topic thus became the relation of intelligence test scores to specialization in the arts and sciences; and I was shipped off to Cambridge to pursue it, there being no one in the Oxford Institute whose interests encompassed a topic so remote from psychological respectability. I was in fact exchanged for Anne Treisman, a person of charm and academic distinction, now renowned for her work on selective attention. The exchange was described at the time – in Oxford, but not in Cambridge – as 'a good swop'.

An interest in intelligence met none of the requirements of scientific respectability: it was macrocosmic rather than microcosmic; its techniques were paper-and-pencil rather than electronic; and it was tarred with the brush of 'education'. It also implied an immersion in statistics, viewed in Cambridge at that time as something done in London. I would like to be able to record that my attitude was one of defiance. In fact, it was craven. For fully a year, I could not bring myself to confess to my peers in grace what my Ph.D. topic was; and instead of swallowing self-respect and getting down to practicalities, I effected an uneasy compromise. As a consequence my first year in research was largely wasted, and in the shallows of the pool in which Anne Treisman has since swum with such conviction. I made photographic slides of patterns of dots; and cloistered in a blacked-out junk room of the Cambridge Laboratory, I flashed these patterns in front of girls from the local teachers' training college. After much effort and calculation, I proved that a currently favoured aspect of information theory, one of almost total vacuity, gave rise to predictions that were false; false, that is, if the theory was interpreted as I chose to interpret it. In the hearty jargon of experimental psychology, the whole effort was judged 'bi-spherical'. Happily I published nothing, and this aspect of information theory has passed into oblivion; entombed on the walls of libraries, in volumes that only the historians of human error will now read.

However, there was one useful outcome of that first year. Casually, over tea one day, Oliver Zangwill remarked to two of us that he could not understand why no one had looked systematically at the academic records of famous scientists. We hurried off to the University Library and did so. What we found surprised us; and, at the time, surprised almost everyone else as well. We traced the undergraduate careers of Fellows of the Royal Society and of Doctors of Science at Oxford and Cambridge. At Cambridge at least, their degrees were no better than those of their contemporaries in research. Under a covering note from the professor, this finding was sent to the editor of the journal *Nature*, a gentleman of such austerity that he could then be addressed only in indirect speech. Our letter was published; *The Times* ran a longish column about it; and the *New Scientist* took it upon itself to mention the degree classes of individuals, getting them wrong in almost every case.

The result was surprising because it was assumed that Fellows of the Royal Society, having 'first-rate minds', would automatically have First Class degrees. No one had looked to see whether this assumption was justified, because to look was to doubt, and to doubt was to call one of the sustaining myths of academic life into question. It is there that the chief interest of that particular piece of research now seems to lie. But at the time, I had a more simple-minded view. I believed that research gained its point by being 'valid' in some Platonic sense, rather than by exploring the assumptions about human nature on which our particular brand of social life depends.

Assumptions and expectations are themselves a somewhat Rilkean theme. But his sonnet also bears on that first small success in a quite different way. Until then, research had seemed like schoolwork; at best, a rehearsal or exercise. Mention in *The Times* served to authenticate the work I had done, to make it seem real. The media – television, radio, the more literate news-papers – are now the standard means whereby one academic finds out what his neighbour is doing. Increasingly, we read not the technical literature, but the gloss put upon it by science correspondents, allowing them to sieve for us the important from the more trivial. This habit has its hazards; but it is at least widely acknowledged. The authenticating function of the media, on the other hand, I have rarely seen mentioned. Yet, in a literal sense, few young research workers believe in what they do. They have spent so long in a system of artifice, pre-paring for one kind of examination or another, that when they get into research they cannot accept their own work for what it is: a contribution to the stuff that textbooks are made of. In this sense, the media provide a seal of existential approval. That it should be the shifting, at times shifty, world of journalism that provides this confirmation, the *Mirror* that authenticates the mirrored, is something of an irony, but one that Rilke himself would probably have taken in his stride.

Early in my second year, and with a strong sense of reluct-ance, I eventually buckled down to the business of intelligence test scores. The topic is one with an established, highly statistical research tradition; but one with which neither Oxford nor Cambridge psychologists have had much truck. As a result, my own first efforts were amateurish in the extreme. Cambridge is an insular place, in which, as I hope I have made plain, considerable psychic energy is devoted to the admiration of one's own excellence. Some of the side effects of such self-absorption are obnoxious; others, though, are harmless, or even useful. In my own case, ignorance was distinctly an asset. My objective, technically speaking, was to show that young scientists had a bias, like my own, towards non-verbal reasoning; whilst arts specialists had a bias towards the use of words. Although my supervisor and I were unaware of the fact, American research teams had hammered at this rather unappetizing nut for more than a decade, and with results that were almost entirely negative. As soon as my own evidence was assembled, it was clear that what held for American students did not hold for English. On this side of the Atlantic, differences between the arts and sciences were marked. The explanation of this Anglo-American discrepancy lies, almost certainly, in the early specialization between the arts and sciences that English schools then imposed. In this country, in the 1950s, one had a solid measure of a student's preference: whether he was in an arts or a science sixth form. In contrast, the Americans had no more to go on than the answers to multiple-choice tests that students took in all subjects alike. In short, I was lucky; doubly lucky, because if I had heard of the American work, my own would not have been attempted.

Beginning in this humble way, my research spread gradually from intelligence testing to the neighbouring and more doubtful field of personality. This expansion was cautious. And for the first five years or so, the work was dull, largely because I lacked courage in straying from facts as experimentally defined. Indeed, I was not committed to what I was doing in any serious way until the summer of 1962. The American vogue for creativity was then at its height. Getzels and Jackson had published their book *Creativity and Intelligence*, and I was asked to review it for the *Quarterly Journal of Experimental Psychology*. Their work came as a breath of sanity to a research field stifling in its own expertise. I tried their open-ended tests for myself, hoping that they would serve as measures of students' originality. To my surprise, they acted instead as an excellent predictor of whether boys would specialize in the arts or the physical sciences. In Getzels and Jackson's terms, young British arts specialists turned out to be 'high creatives', young physical scientists to be 'high I.Q.s'. Adapting more neutral terms from the American mental tester Guilford, I named them 'divergers' and 'convergers'. This finding, once more communicated to the editor of *Nature*, brought three-page cables from *Time* and *Newsweek*, interviews on television, and a reputation yet to be lived down as an expert on creativity. And the media once more performed their magic. By the winter of 1962, I was half-way to becoming a committed psychologist, a process completed by the publication of my first book four years later. For the publishing trade, like the media, are potent authenticators of the young and rootless. By the time *Contrary Imaginations* was in the bookshops, I was engaged neck and crop.

In *Contrary Imaginations*, I set out to describe the web of connections into which I had strayed: for convergence and divergence proved to be linked to differences in personality, and both were linked in their turn to differences between the arts and the physical sciences.

Set down baldly, these findings were not particularly exciting. Their interest lay in their detail; in the holes they knocked in artificial, statistically defined conceptions of 'intelligence'; and in the bridges they provided between areas of psychology that had evolved to some extent in mutual isolation – intelligence testing, personality research, and work on career choice.

And, more generally, in what one might call their humanizing tendency, steering a small area of psychology back into some semblance of contact with its proper subject-matter: people. The difficulties such findings posed were considerable, even so; for they demanded just that kind of wide-ranging, synthesizing inference from one set of data to another that experimentally trained psychologists of my generation found it peculiarly alarming to perform.

For autobiographical reasons, *Frames of Mind*, my second book, was more flat-footed, less exuberant, than my first. It was better balanced though, and in two respects more evolved. I had moved, in the course of three years, away from the idea of the individual as a 'programmed' or self-sufficient entity, and towards that of a creature who depends – as he does on food, drink and oxygen – on his transactions with the people about him. Also, I had become interested not only in what the individual does, but in his perception of what he does; not only in his capabilities, but in his perception of what he can do.

As early as 1962 or 1963, having watched clever boys making career choices for some five or six years, I had felt it was time I learnt something of how these choices were seen by the individuals concerned. Precedents existed, and techniques were to hand, yet I was slow to get started, and for a familiar reason. Such work seemed vaguely 'bogus'. It belonged, or seemed then to belong, beyond the pale of scientific respectability – along with hypnotism, ESP, LSD, marriage research, sociology, sex research and all other unspecified forms of academic self-indulgence and impropriety. This, despite the fact that such work offered all the trimmings of scientific rigour: large samples, copious statistics, and definable stimulus and response. It somehow seemed beneath the salt.

Questions of respectability aside, there was also a good practical reason for feeling uneasy. I had at the time, and have retained, a Luddite's distaste for punch cards, counter sorters, computers. Yet the kind of study I then envisaged was scarcely practicable without such aids. I proceeded, however, in the best gentlemanly tradition, with paper, pencil and slide-rule. And as each of the 390 boys in my first study made 300 judgments, I had over 100,000 responses to handle. I nearly drowned.*

A good deal of that analysis eventually found its way on to the printed page; and one particular feature still holds a special interest for me – a loose end that acted as a stimulus for the round of research on which I am now engaged. Comparing my own with American results, it was clear that the scientist was perceived generally, on this side of the Atlantic, as on the other, as intelligent but cold, dependable but dull, valuable but lacking in imagination. The arts specialist in contrast was seen as warm but undependable, exciting but relatively unintelligent, imaginative but lacking in value. These were preconceptions shared by young arts and science specialists alike. And at least as far as the 'image' of the scientist was concerned, they were stable from one age level to another. They were nearly as pronounced among able young boys of eleven, innocent of all science, as they were among seventeen-year-olds, whose career pattern was already to some extent determined. In fact, one had the impression that the notion of science and its attendant image entered children's minds almost simultaneously. No sooner did a boy learn how to use the noun 'scientist', than he associated with it adjectives like 'dependable', 'intelligent', 'cold'. On the other hand, with figures from the arts – novelist, poet, artist – this was not so. Whereas the stereotype of the scientist existed fully fledged in the minds of pre-adolescent boys, the stereotype of the artist took shape only slowly as adolescence progressed.

Although I remarked on this oddity in *Frames of Mind*, I

---

* Although irrational, this fear of instant calculation has its compensations. Most social scientists who rely on punch cards and computers seem in practice to abandon their powers of reasoning, and as a result, their data are almost invariably under-analysed, or analysed in a clumsy, ham-fisted fashion. The research worker seems subtly to become the creature of the data-processing machinery, rather than vice versa.

4. An Oxford philosopher of the 1950s, J. L. Austin

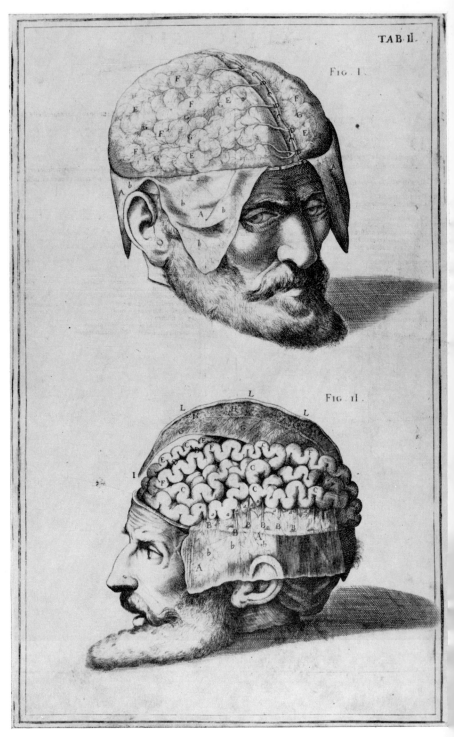

5. A seventeenth-century dissection of the cerebral cortex. One of the first steps towards the 'objective' view of Man. By J. Casserius

could not then see what to make of it. It seemed no more than a tantalizing loose end. More recently, in the light of two new studies, it has begun to slip into place. I will mention both briefly, because they exemplify a more integrated and more biographical approach to the study of human intelligence. Each, on the face of it, may seem a little far-fetched: the first concerning patterns of marriage and fertility among eminent academics, the second centring on the question of whether convergers are as likely as divergers to recall the contents of their dreams. Superficially, the three topics – stereotypes, marriage and fertility, and dreaming – are totally unrelated, except perhaps as divergencies from a central theme. They knit together, even so.

The marriage study was one that I did, appropriately enough, in collaboration with my wife; and it was based on that strange volume, *Who's Who*.[1] It was designed to test our belief that the type of intelligence a man chooses to display in his working life is linked systematically to the kind of personal life he leads. The results were impressive. We found, for example, that a remarkable proportion of scholars in the arts had no children at all, either because they remained single, or because they had childless marriages. They also tended to marry late, but were unlikely to divorce. In contrast, most of the eminent scientists in *Who's Who* had married. The biologists had often done so late; also, they tended to have large families, and were surprisingly susceptible to divorce. The physical scientists, in contrast, had more modest families, and, with the exception of the physicists, divorced only rarely. Social scientists were unfortunately a small and diverse group, but their divorce rate appeared to be high. Novelists, playwrights and poets had few children, and seemed to be single, married and divorced in roughly equal proportions.

The dream research was carried out by a research student of mine, Mark Austin; and its results too have been clear-cut.

When convergers and divergers are subjected to the rigours of the sleep laboratory, they appear, physiologically speaking, to dream to the same extent. Their patterns, both of rapid eye movement and of electrical activity in the brain associated with dreaming, are much the same. Yet the groups differ in what they recall. If divergers are woken in the midst of rapid eye movement sleep, they almost invariably recall dreaming, and the dreams they recall are in every sense abundant. Convergers, in contrast, are quite likely to recall dreaming, but not *what* they were dreaming; or to recall nothing at all.[2]

The threads of meaning that connect these two pieces of research with each other, and with the earlier finding about stereotypes, grew first, as far as I was concerned, from an article about music by Anthony Storr, in which he touched on the 'latency' period in children's development:

> One of its most interesting and least studied features is the opportunity it gives the child to develop passions for ideas, symbols, and abstractions instead of people. It is likely that the greatest cultural achievements of man rest upon predilections acquired between the ages of five and thirteen.[3]

In rough-and-ready terms, growing up can be divided into three phases – infancy, childhood and adolescence – and the latency period is associated with the second of these. The years from 'five to thirteen' can thus be seen as those in which the individual asserts control over his more infantile impulses, in order that he may be free to explore the external world. Adolescence, in contrast, can be envisaged as a phase in which he discovers, or rediscovers, life's emotional, interpersonal, erotic possibilities. In terms of broadest generality, the latency period can be seen as a phase concerned with emotional control; and adolescence as one concerned with emotional rediscovery. The connection with my first set of results, those about stereotypes, is now easier to see, though still hard to formulate in any precise way. The stereotype that takes shape during the latency period, that of the scientist, itself embodies ideas of emotion control; the stereotype that takes shape in adolescence – that of the artist – embodies those of emotional self-expression. It seems, in other words, that the values that go to define the scientific and artistic ways of life may reflect the psychic processes dominant in their respective developmental stages. What these psychic processes are is made a little less obscure by the work on dreaming.

Austin's demonstration of the difference in dream recall between convergers and divergers is, as far as I know, the first to bear directly and experimentally on the mental processes that underlie adult work. The implication is that, among convergers, the control of emotional expression is not a matter of personal choice, or conscious decision, but a pervasive feature of their mental life. Where divergers are more open to the irrational elements in their own mental functioning, convergers tend intuitively, automatically, to block these elements out. In a word, they repress them. If late infancy and early childhood are seen as the period during which the child starts to stake out his sense of who he is – to delineate the character he will in future present to himself, and to the world at large – the results on dream recall fall into place. Convergers can be envisaged as children who construct robust 'ego-boundaries', and include within them only what is rational. Divergers, in contrast, form relatively weak ego-boundaries and allow their own irrational impulses to suffuse their perception of who they are. The model is one I used in *Contrary Imaginations*, and I was in this sense familiar with it. Its relevance was sharpened, though, by reading an article on emotional expression among young American mathematicians, psychologists and poets.[4] The mathematicians followed the convergent pattern, the poets the divergent – the psychologists providing an interesting variant: they seemed to have established strong ego-boundaries, like the mathematicians; yet seemed, unlike the mathematicians, to be committed to colonize the irrational world that lay without.*

The identity of convergent and divergent children can be seen, in other words, as crystallizing to differing extents and at different stages: the convergent during the latency period, the divergent in adolescence. The internal economy of the convergent child, the future scientist, might be said to gel at the stage in his development when issues of rationality and internal control are paramount. That of the divergent child, the future arts specialist, sets less firmly, and at a stage when emotional considerations are again more pressing. The convergent child fixates early, on the only constellation of values then available; the divergent child delays, homing eventually on the second constellation of values, the artistic one, which is antithetic to the first.

From such a simple model, a number of predictions flow. If a child fixates early, one would expect him to choose work that is impersonal; to show a limited capacity for introspection and emotional response to people; to be conventional; to be dissociated in his expression of sexuality; to separate clearly his working life from his private life; and to work harmoniously in groups. In contrast, one would expect the child who fixates relatively late to choose work involving people; to show greater capacity for introspection and emotional reponse; to have relatively little reliance on social conventions; to show a freer, and more integrated, pattern of sexuality; to separate his private life from his work relatively little; and to have difficulty in working in groups. One could also go on to win from the model some of the more apparently paradoxical aspects of the

---

* The account given by Hoffberg and Fast in this article of the psychic lives of young poets, based on the analysis of responses to projective tests, agrees remarkably well with biographical descriptions of Rilke.

differences between the arts and the sciences. The longer the delay in fixation, the greater the distance – both in time and psychically – between the establishment of a socially present-able self and the untrammelled expression of impulse that characterizes infancy. Hence one would expect what one often seems to find: that the converger, though conventional, is more capable than the diverger of *authentic* emotional response.* In contrast, the late fixator, the diverger, will tend to have re-created his impulsive life in intellectual terms, and to respond, especially in crises, in ways that are at once florid and hollow. One would also expect that the divergent child, being less clearly formed, would experience more turbulence in adoles-cence than the converger; and that he would be more likely than the converger to throw himself into social life in a disruptive way, pursuing his autobiography at his institution's expense.

The remaining piece of evidence, that about marriage and fertility, fits quite well into this pattern. The marital lives of physical scientists – early 'fixators', one presumes – are on the whole more conventional than those either of biological scientists, or of scholars in the arts. This, on the other hand, is a paraphrase. There are many more detailed features of these results which the model will not predict: differences, for example, between physicists and chemists, between scholars in the arts and creative writers. The model, in other words, is only a beginning. But this is as it should be, otherwise one would be led to explain reductively, describing vastly complex ecological processes entirely in terms of single organisms and their internal states.

The interrelation of the private and the public, the individual and the social, becomes plain in a study we have made recently

* Bronfenbrenner has noticed how controlled Russian children are in comparison with American children, but how free they are to express affection to the young. He describes his son of four being 'scooped up, hugged and resoundingly kissed' by a party of teenage Russian boys. As he says, 'Similar behaviour on the part of any American adolescent male would surely prompt his parents to consult a psychiatrist.'[5]

of young research students and their wives. One of our strongest impressions is that the choice these young men have made of a wife has played a crucial part in crystallizing their attitudes, and the patterns of life they are to follow. Not only did the young married physical scientists in our sample differ biographically from, say, the biologists; they differed sharply in the kinds of girl they married, and the kinds of relationship that ensued. In certain respects, in fact, the wives of physical scientists differ more from other wives than do the physical scientists themselves from other husbands. And the wives differ not only in their beliefs, but in such seemingly basic, biological respects as the age at which they reached sexual maturity. It has also been salutary to discover that these differences – whilst broadly confirming the 'early fixation' hypothesis – run in a number of respects counter to the stereotype of the dull physical scientist and his dowdy bride.

Evidence of broader historical and cultural influences on the individual is equally easy to find. In the *Who's Who* study, for example, there were signs that rates of divorce were high in an academic discipline when it was in a state of intellectual ferment, low when it was more nearly quiescent. And in an extension of the *Who's Who* work to include the medical profession, we found evidence that medical specialization was influenced to a remarkable extent by considerations of social class. Specialities which enjoy high professional esteem are on the whole more likely than others to draw their eminent members from secondary schools in England as opposed to Scotland, Wales or Northern Ireland, and from private schools as opposed to state schools. Consultant surgeons and physicians, for example, were more likely than, say, pharmacologists or dentists, to have come from private schools in England.

Such niceties can be traced out in remarkable detail – yet in ways which cannot be explained entirely in terms of social or medical snobbery. For specialists from English private schools are more likely than others to achieve eminence by working on living bodies, as opposed to dead bodies; on the head, as opposed to the lower trunk; on the surface of the body, as opposed to its insides; and on male bodies, as opposed to female. The eminent British physician is more likely, for instance, to have been to an English private school than is an eminent anatomist; the ear nose and throat specialist than the gastro-intestinal surgeon; the dermatologist than the pathologist; the urologist than the gynaecologist. These are results that defy analysis in terms of medical skill; on the other hand, they carry an obvious anthropological implication – it is precisely such categories as these that structuralists like Lévi-Strauss have elicited from the analysis of the myths and rituals of economically primitive societies. Parts of the body, evidently, possess symbolic significance – a significance that influences medical students when they are deciding to specialize. And, it would seem, students from an upper-middle-class background are more likely than those from a lower-middle or working-class background to find their way into specialities that are seen for symbolic reasons as desirable.

In practice, of course, the psychological, social and cultural interdepend. For people do not merely interact, bumping into one another like billiard-balls; they perceive and form expectations of one another, and cling for life and sanity to the confirmation that their immediate neighbours provide. As Erving Goffman has it, there is 'no agent more effective than another person in bringing a world for oneself alive, or, by a glance, a gesture, or a remark, shrivelling up the reality in which one is lodged'.[6] And obviously, too, in a general way, Rilke's sonnet has a bearing on such matters. Like Goffman, Rilke deals with the potency of human expectations. On the other hand, if this were all he was saying, there is no reason why his sonnet should have been so disruptive to me. His proposition is compatible with the experiments I described in *Frames of Mind*; and, in fact, in a gnomic fashion, serves to epitomize them. Beyond question, there was an incompatibility, though. This arose, I now believe, not from the details of what I was doing, but from the covert metaphors or models of human nature and of rational inquiry that informed it. I was shifting ground, I think successfully, to reconcile my assumptions about human nature with those of the social scientists I was getting to know; but my view of knowledge itself was more deeply entrenched.

And it is here, I am now sure, that the real source of disruption lay. In his sonnet, Rilke deals not only in expectation and belief, but in myth; in symbols that convey intuitively perceived meanings, themselves the outcome of the lengthy processes of cultural accretion. Rilke's unicorn and virgin are quite remote from the data a psychologist or sociologist could now produce. And in using them to convey his meaning, he disregards totally the empirically trained scientist's besetting anxieties about evidence. If, as sceptics, we were to ask Rilke to define his terms, and to provide objective data in support of his proposition, we would be philistines – because we would be attempting not merely to dismantle his poem, but also to stifle both its meaning and the experience it embodies.

To find a philosophy of research that could do no violence of this kind is a lofty and perhaps misguided ambition. But to cling blindly to the particular philosophy one has been taught is unintelligent; and to look for less clumsy alternatives is not misguided at all. The prospect is a little intimidating, even so; for it opens out into a no-man's-land where there are not textbooks to guide one.

The Radical Objection 5

I was brought up to believe that ideas were potent inasmuch as they were logical, sharply defined. I now realize that this is not a self-evident truth, but is itself an attitude or point of view. And experience of academic life points, if in any direction, in the opposite one: to the view that, at least among men who believe that they are rational, ideas are more powerful the vaguer they become; and that their power inheres, in some curious way, in their very inexplicitness. Chief among these nebulous notions is that of being either 'soft' or 'hard'. The psychology I learnt at Oxford, and the ideals of research prevalent in Cambridge, were both unequivocally 'hard'. Behaviouristic psychology, in general, is 'tough-minded', 'hard-nosed', 'hard'. And the position of 'hard' psychology in British universities over the last thirty years has been overwhelmingly strong.

None the less, there has been opposition, and over the last five years or so this has grown increasingly vociferous. Fifteen years ago, the vast majority of those working in psychological departments here and in the United States shared the belief that their discipline was robust, that their efforts embodied the onward march of Science. However, in the early 1960s, a number of the informed and eminent, Sigmund Koch, for instance, were making sounds of misgiving, suggesting that for reasons of scientific insecurity psychology was in retreat from its 'historically constituted subject-matter'. Koch went on to say something even more important, although it passed largely unheeded at the time:

That modern psychology has projected an image of man which is as demeaning as it is simplistic, few intelligent and sensitive non-psychologists would deny. To such men – whether they be scientist, humanist, or citizen – psychology has increasingly become an object of derision. *They* are safe, even when most despairing. But for the rest, the mass dehumanization process which characterizes our time – the simplification of sensibility, the homogenization of taste, attenuation of the capacity for experience – continues apace. Of all fields in the community of scholarship, it should be psychology which combats this trend. Instead, we have played no small role in augmenting and supporting it.[1]

The message was plain enough: in its drive to be scientifically respectable, psychology had not merely become trivial; it was contributing to a tide, perhaps an irreversible tide, of social mischief. Yet at the time Koch was writing, information theory was still the rage in experimental departments in this country. It had yet to be succeeded, belatedly, by enthusiasm for the work of the Harvard behaviourist, Skinner, who toured the United Kingdom in the mid-1960s, and bowled many of us over with his contempt both for theory and for statistics, and his zeal for moulding or 'shaping up' the behaviour of the individual organism. (He had taught pigeons to play table-tennis – a remarkable feat, if a little barren – by skilful use of rewards.) Yet, paradoxically, it was at just this point that confidence in the scientific approach to psychology in this country began to falter. A shift in the *Zeitgeist* had occurred, unmistakable if unexplained. What had seemed self-evidently true, suddenly became a matter of personal opinion, even of prejudice. What had struck one as elegant, was now in danger of seeming pointless. As early as 1956, Zangwill had had the prescience to write: 'Experimental psychology has produced many facts, a few generalisations, and even an occasional "law". But it has so far failed to produce anything resembling a coherent and generally accepted body of scientific theory.'[2] On the other side of the Atlantic, and more recently on this side, self-doubting articles began to appear in the house journals of professional psychologists, the *American Psychologist* and the *Bulletin of the British Psychological Society*, with such titles as 'On the Need for Relativism', 'Fads, Fashions and Folderol in Psychology', 'The Breakdown of Modern Psychology,' 'Psychopathologies: Syndromes of an Ailing Profession'. And, simultaneously, attacks from without, for instance from the linguist Noam Chomsky, acquired a less forlorn and more penetrating tone. Within the space of a few years, our infatuation with hard science seems, somewhat abruptly, to have collapsed. And books which presaged this – notably, for example, Norman Brown's strange, fertile work *Life Against Death* – somewhat neglected when first published, are now being read by psychologists with close attention:*

> There is an attack on the great god Science in psychoanalysis; but the nature of the attack needs careful explanation. What is being probed, and found to be in some sense morbid, is not knowledge as such, but the unconscious schemata governing the pursuit of knowledge in modern civilization – specifically the aim of possession or mastery over objects, and the principle of economizing in the means. And the morbidity imputed to these schemata, if interpreted in the context of the whole libido theory, amounts to this: possessive mastery over nature and rigorously economical thinking are partial impulses in the human being

---

* *Life Against Death* was neglected, too, by radicals because its publication coincided with that of Marcuse's *Eros and Civilisation*. Both are expositions and reconciliations of Freud's thought with Marx's. Marcuse's is much the more reductively political in tone; and, partly for this reason, is in my judgment much the less stimulating book of the two.

(the human body) which in modern civilization have become tyrant organizers of the whole of human life ... [3]

This impulse towards 'quantifying rationality', Brown sees not
as an error but as a 'disease in consciousness'; a matter not of the
'conscious structure' of science, but its 'unconscious premises'.
To know about nature, and especially about people, in a way
that reduces them to thing-hood, is to pursue knowledge in a
way that is inimical to the proper growth of human self-
awareness.*

In the British Isles, disillusionment of a radical kind has
crystallized to a remarkable extent around the work of a single
man: Ronald Laing. Over the last five years, his books have
probably had more impact on the minds of intelligent British
students than has the rest of psychology put together.

The Laingian corpus is conceived within the Continental
tradition that most Englishmen of my generation and older
find alien. He admires Sartre, not Wittgenstein. He starts, as
Chomsky has urged we must, and as Descartes started long ago,
from the integrating capabilities of the human mind, rather
than from the observable elements of human behaviour. From
what is whole rather than fragmented, hidden rather than
displayed for the impartial observer to observe. His conception
of psychology is so remote from the one I pursued in Cambridge
that, comparing them, it is hard to believe that they can have
even a verbal label – 'psychology' – in common. They address
different problems, and do so by different routes. One aligns
itself with existentialism and phenomenology; attempts to
describe the influence of our minds on our actions; and
accepts that all issues of substance are issues of perceived
meaning. The other stems, or at least is usually said to stem,

---

* Simultaneously, in the mid-1960s, an analogous movement occurred among
sociologists: against the assumption that the sociologist is a 'scientist', that his work is
'value free'.[4]

from the English empiricism of Locke and Hume; it sets itself to formulate laws of behaviour rather than of experience; and the only meanings it countenances are those that one man ascribes to the behaviour of another.

Laing's work appeals for a number of reasons, some more profound than others. First of all, he is assured. He is also eloquent; sometimes he preaches, in the declamatory style of the conscience-scouring Scottish cleric; but often he writes as well as anyone could wish to. He is passionately involved in what he describes. He is neither a philistine nor a bland optimist, being one of a few British psychologists of recent years to give both the subtleties and distortions of human experience their due. He talks about what goes on in people's minds, what people do to each other's minds; and is prepared to speak of human suffering, and the human capacity for evil. (In contrast, behavioural psychology has the hollowly optimistic air of an anodyne, of movement towards a brave new future, which now seems its most dated feature.) But the simplest, most influential reason of all, I suspect, is that Laing is not a be-haviourist – the enthusiasm for Laingian psychology being a phenomenon that the crudities of behaviourism have done much to create.

Some years ago, at the time I was writing *Contrary Imagina-tions*, I had high hopes of a reconciliation between the Laingian and the experimental schools of thought. Both, I argued, would end in sterility if pursued in isolation. But no such rapproche-ment has occurred. The experimentalists have noticed with alarm that Laing can speak across their heads to their students; and some, as a result, have adopted defensive postures, preparing to fight for what they see as the scientific decencies. Others, while retaining their links with the empirical tradition, are becoming more exploratory and less dogmatic.*

* A significant detail, among even the hardest of the hard, is their abandonment of the Watsonian label 'behaviourist'. They are now calling themselves 'empiricists' instead.

Laing and his followers have moved more rapidly, but in the opposite direction; and as a result the gap between the two positions, rather than narrowing, has widened. In his first two books, *The Divided Self* and *The Self and Others*, published in 1959 and 1960, Laing delineated and described with great subtlety. Five years later, in *Sanity, Madness and the Family*, he did the same, rather more factually. In *Interpersonal Perception*, published in 1966, he discussed techniques. Even this late, paths seemed still to be converging. But in *The Politics of Experience*, which came out in 1967, the gulf opened once more, and is opening still. For here, he is not merely describing, he is explaining; and at times, to my eye at least, explaining away. All forms of human suffering and inadequacy now seem to have been laid at the door of manipulative parents and the corrupting social order. Behind humanity's presenting symptoms, he, like Marcuse, sees the greater evil of the military-industrial complex. The causes he postulates are political, sociological, and simple.

More recently still, in *Knots*, Laing's style likewise has changed, being now as much poetic as factual; so in this respect, too, he has moved away from the conventionally scientific rather than towards it. Whilst applauding his versatility, and admiring much of what he has written without reservation, I view the evolution in his thought with some misgiving. Evolution, though, it unquestionably is; and where Laing, Marcuse and Jules Henry have led, a substantial part of the student body has followed.

Since 1965, I have done my best to practise what *Contrary Imaginations* preached. Whilst remaining an empiricist in method – my data are usually as hard as the next man's, or nearly so – I have edged continually towards those areas of experience that softer, more humane psychologists and sociologists have seen as vital. And distantly echoing the Continental structuralists, whose endeavour I seem largely – and fortunately – to have misunderstood, I have begun to look for systems of intuitive meaning that will lend my data shape.* Such work is pleasant to do, but less than entirely satisfying. And this is so, I think, because psychology itself contains opposed systems of intuitive meaning that make the task of reconciliation especially difficult. For, looking back on it, *Frames of Mind* has an agnostic air. It is a book that lacks any single, all-embracing credo to unite it and give it direction. However artificial or implausible such credos may be, they give research a good *Gestalt.*† In comparison, the agnostic is a dull dog. He may be lively in passing, but he lacks that primitive conviction that persuades others, and hence himself, that what he is doing is momentous. He lacks even the self-righteous glow that forthright atheism creates. In comparison with the zealot, interdisciplinary man is more a person of kapok, of wadding. And by stepping out of a clear tradition, out of the framework that the divisions between academic subjects create, he can also leave himself feeling vulnerable; perhaps, as the structuralists have suggested, because cultural labels, categories and rituals are the props on which the ordinary mortal's sense of identity is hung.

In contemplating this book, I had hoped to track the hard and soft traditions in psychology to source; to trace their historical origins in Anglo-Saxon and Continental philosophy respectively, and then to play one off against the other, in Hegelian fashion, creating as I did so a model that would lend an interdisciplinary approach just that primitive coherence it now lacks. Without doubt, the hard and the soft, the Anglo-Saxon and the Continental traditions, are distinct. And Chomsky has argued, forcefully, that we cannot understand the present state of the

---

* The structuralists' programme – of banishing 'the subject' and all issues of perceived meaning and value from scholarly discourse – has a disastrous precedent in strict, behavioural psychology. There, research has acted as a screen or front behind which personal ideologies – like Skinner's, for example – are pursued unrestrainedly.

† Recent ethological work based on the conceit that the school-child is like the chimpanzee, and can be studied as though he were one, has about it an air of quite spurious elegance that research treating children as children usually lacks.

human sciences unless we take their historical evolution into account. He is probably right; but schools of thought within psychology, though broadly aligned with philosophical traditions, seem in detail to draw on a bewildering variety of sources. And the sources themselves are often interwoven and confused, even within the work of a single man.

The scientific approach to psychology, for example, on which I was weaned, was imported into this country from the United States after the Second World War. It had flourished there since the 1920s, and had drawn in equal parts, or so it now seems, on the pragmatic hostility to metaphysics epitomized by the thought of Peirce and Dewey, and on the evangelical, fundamentalist tradition we now associate with Billy Graham. But it had reached the United States not from England, but from Germany: the land of Hegel, the home of metaphysics and phenomenology.

The Anglo-Saxon tradition in philosophy is likewise richly confused. Locke and Hume, and for that matter, Russell and Ayer, though empiricists, and preoccupied with the question of evidence, are concerned with sense data in ways that modern behaviourists find antipathetic. Conversely the philosopher who most clearly embodies the behaviouristic vision – Man as a Machine – was not an Anglo-Saxon at all, but a Frenchman: La Mettrie. English empiricism has largely been atomistic, but it is by no means the only atomistic philosophy: Locke's perception of knowledge is of the 'building-block' kind, but so too – as I understand it – is that of the archetypal Continental rationalist Leibniz. Locke conceived of the human mind as a *tabula rasa*, a clean slate; so too do behaviourists, like Watson and Skinner.[5] But other hard psychologists follow Galton, and argue powerfully for the influence of genetics. The rationalist Descartes asserted the existence of innate ideas. Chomsky, a vigorous opponent of behaviourism, has followed him; but most of the more humane, and more sociological, psychologists seem, like Laing, to envisage a Lockean clean slate. Nearer home, the analytic, linguistic philosophy that I learnt at Oxford, and which echoes in many ways the tones of behaviourist psychology, had its origins not among Anglo-Saxons, but in Vienna and the work of Carnap and Schlick.

Allegiances within psychology, then, are not historical, at least in the sense that they can be laid bare in a retrospective review. They are real, none the less. And some studies of my own – the ones I have touched on already, dealing with the image of the artist and the scientist – seem to offer an insight into their nature. It is to these that I would like to turn next.

The Soft and the Hard   6

One of the strongest features of the stereotyped ideas surrounding the arts and sciences is the split they embody between ideas
of pleasure and ideas of value. Artist, poet and novelist are all
seen in my studies as warm and exciting, but as of little worth.
Mathematician, physicist and engineer are all seen as extremely
valuable, but also as dull and cold. It is clear, too, that the arts
are associated with sexual pleasure, the sciences with sexual
restraint. The arts man is seen as having a good-looking,
well-dressed wife with whom he enjoys a warm sexual
relation; the scientist as having a wife who is dowdy and dull,
and in whom he has no physical interest. Yet the scientist
is seen as masculine, the arts specialist as slightly feminine. So
it seems that masculinity is associated in schoolboys' minds
now, just as it was in the minds of Victorian moralists, with
sexual abstinence, whilst effeminacy in men is associated with
licence.*

Such popular oppositions of meaning are not the whole
of human life, nor, for that matter, the whole of meaning;
but they do seem to provide the framework within which
more detailed, and apparently more rational judgments are
made. They represent the presuppositions and prejudices into
which we lapse. Their power to seduce us is illustrated by a
small experiment of my own. This centred on the 'Uses of
Objects' test, one which invites you to suggest as many uses as

* Student at Keele University, quoted in *Financial Times*, January 1969: 'The trouble
with taking science in university is that you spend all afternoon in a laboratory, while
your girl's in bed with an arts man.'

you can for certain everyday objects. The individual is free to answer as he chooses – for many, a unique educational experience. Yet normally, I know within quite narrow margins of error how many uses a given group of boys in a given school will produce. On this particular occasion, I had before me boys I had already tested once, four months earlier. This second time, they were invited to perform two charades: to pretend, first, that they were Robert Higgins, a successful computer engineer; and then, John McMice, a well-known artist. Higgins was established as a dedicated, conscientious man, with a logical mind and a gift for gadgets. He was shy but friendly, and had a dislike for woolly ideas and any show of personal emotion. He caricatured, in other words, the image of the physical scientist – and, incidentally, the image of the experimental psychologist that the experimental psychologists themselves project. McMice, in contrast, was described as uninhibited and rather Bohemian, as someone who said things for effect, and had a tendency to shock people with coarse or gruesome jokes.

Seventy fifteen-year-olds took part. The setting: the examination hall of a renowned public boarding-school, portraits of previous headmasters looking down on us all, weighty, and in some cases lugubrious. The boys sat as for an examination, in rows, with ample space between them. I stood at the front, busying myself with piles of paper. Each boy was asked to put his name on his answer sheet and did so. There was no other adult present.

The curious quality of this occasion lay in the ease with which the boys adopted the two masks: the scientist and the artist. In the case of McMice, some of the answers were of a violence and obscenity that bewilders me still. I find it hard to credit that fifteen-year-old boys, especially boys from a school of such intense respectability, should reveal themselves so openly on so slender an excuse. Higgins and McMice were *personae* that seemed to float to the surface of their minds quite naturally, and their responses flowed more smoothly in the majority of cases than had the responses that the boys had been willing, four months earlier, to identify as their own.

In *Frames of Mind*, I used this experiment to advance a particular view of how the human psyche functions. That we have inside us a number of separate selves, some of which are on display, while others see the light of day rarely, appearing like strangers only in circumstances that are exceptional. I also suggested, following Jung, that the public self may counterbalance others that are less acceptable. On this argument, our public face bears only a complicated relation to our more private faces; and the more forceful the expression of a public self, the more curious about such internal relations the onlooker may reasonably become.

Obviously, the argument applies equally to the images we develop collectively; and the position of the psychologist proves in this respect intriguing. For able boys see him as a figure more akin to the artist than to the scientist. He is seen as imaginative, exciting, smooth, unmanly, somewhat lazy, and as lacking in value. His only scientific quality is his high intelligence. Boys attribute to him, in other words, the life of the pleasure-seeker: the life that both Hercules and the physical scientist are thought, in terms of their respective myths, to have renounced in favour of 'toil and glory'.

What strikes one here is the sharp discontinuity between this perception of psychology, and the view of matters propagated by our university teaching departments. There, in the course of three years, the students' perception of psychology is stood on its head. They enter expecting to study a subject that is humane, and emerge convinced that it is a science. That such a feat of inculcation is possible is remarkable in itself. And it should scarcely surprise us if it leaves behind a residue of dissatisfaction.

Where a teaching department's projection of a professional identity is unusually insistent, one's impulse, whether or not one has truck with Jungian ideas, is to look for sources of professional anxiety. In the case of psychology these are not hard to find. Psychologists have a marginal position in the academic community, poised near the borderline between the humane and the scientific disciplines; we have a farouche professional past, redolent of mesmerism, even of witch-doctoring; and there still exist widespread misgivings – both in academic life and in society at large – about any attempt to examine the mind's contents. Our response, professionally, has been to over-react: to observe all the outward signs of scientific respectability, taking as our model, incidentally, the Victorian conception of the physical scientist, a model that physical scientists themselves have long abandoned. Here, as elsewhere, one has the impression of a professional group plunging, in search of an identity, from one extreme to another. A sense of orderly growth is lacking; and so too is any awareness that urgently propounded theses usually carry their own negation buried within them.

Before relinquishing questions of professional identity, I would like to turn back to the adjectives hard and soft; and to do a little more delving. In science, their currency is universal: a shorthand that almost all of us use in describing each other's position; and in psychology, as I have said, the physiological and technological traditions are accepted as hard, the intuitive and more humane as soft. The essential feature of the first is its preoccupation with behaviour: with the organism – its physical, corporeal presence, and what it can be seen to do. The essential feature of the second is its emphasis on personal relationships and on the world of experience. The terms hard and soft, within psychology, thus have a philosophical implication: they bear on the Cartesian distinction between body and mind. Demonstrably, too, as we have seen, hard and soft are closely linked semantically with a number of other notions. Soft is associated, not just with the arts as opposed to science and the animate as opposed to the inanimate; but with mind rather than body; with feminity rather than masculinity; with pleasure-seeking rather than abstinence; and with the valueless rather than the valuable. Arguably perhaps, too, it carries with it connotations of social class – certainly, in the *Who's Who* study, scholars in the arts turned out to be massively more likely than the physical scientists to have come from private schools.

These values cluster in ways that, if mysterious, are at least consistent. But why? Why should it be manly and valuable to concern oneself with behaviour, feminine and less valuable to concern oneself with experience; hard, to work on the inert, soft on the living? The answer perhaps lies in a general tendency, embracing not only our own culture but also others, for males to adopt one area of social responsibility and females another. Ethnographic evidence about primitive people suggests, overwhelmingly, that it is the men who wage war, hunt animals, and wield political authority. Women are more domestic and more nurturative. Evidence from more sophisticated societies, the kibbutzim for example, points to an analogous pattern. One such area of male domination in our own society is physical science. In Britain and the United States, women in the physical sciences are unusual; in engineering and technology, rare. Like the physical sciences, though to a lesser extent, experimental psychology is dominated by men. The softer areas, in contrast, are more attractive to women – one notices this particularly in teaching at the undergraduate level. Again, though, why?

Some insight into this arbitrary-seeming demarcation may be found in the distinction that sociologists draw between 'instrumental' and 'expressive' approaches to social life and to thought. The instrumental approach is one essentially concerned with the impersonal control, the subjugation, of the environment; the expressive with relationships between one person and another. Some men, obviously, are predominantly expressive; some women, instrumental. And all of us vary along this dimension from time to time, and place to place. But the demands that our society places on men, and the patterns of adaptation they engender, are for the most part clearly instrumental; and those on women, predominantly expressive. It is the instrumental qualities, the concern with impersonal control, that we normally describe as hard. And in psychology – or so the interpretation runs – the behavioural tradition is seen as hard, because it treats people for all practical purposes as objects, and aims to subjugate them, in instrumental fashion, to relatively simple laws. The more humane traditions are seen as soft inasmuch as they treat people as people, and are concerned less with law-making than with speculative exploration. Even so, there remains a great deal to explain. Why, for example, should the notions of masculinity and instrumentality be associated with self-control and sexual abstinence?

Such questions are sometimes easiest to grasp in historical and literary terms. Virility, it is easy to forget in these less stringent times, was the quality that Victorians especially prized. It was virility that gave a man 'that consciousness of his dignity, of his character as head and ruler, and of his importance, which is absolutely essential to the well-being of the family, and through it of society itself'.[1] This happy state was achieved through self-control. Victorian moralists and doctors alike – the gynaecologist Acton, for example – took as their premise the belief that virility was endangered by any loss of semen; though the worst threats to health and the moral order could be avoided if intercourse was indulged in only rarely. Sexual indulgence, especially among the young, was thought to lead inexorably to physical deterioration and insanity. And it is clear from what Acton wrote, that he for one linked sexual freedom in the young male with effeminacy. It is not, in his phrase, the 'strong athletic boy, fond of healthy exercise, who thus early shows marks of sexual desires, but your puny exotic, whose intellectual education has been fostered at the expense of his physical development'.[2]

Paradoxically, although Victorians like Acton viewed women-like men as soft and licentious, women themselves – the well-bred ones – were assumed to be sexually inert. As Wayland Young has said, 'About men, Acton writes like a bluffly affectionate elder brother, warning, exhorting, even from time to time forgiving. About women he writes like a vet.'[3] This categorical exclusion of women aside, the Victorian conception of virility can be seen as a metaphor drawn from economics; it is the state of a male organism that has hoarded its limited sexual resources. Virility equalled frugality, equalled self-denial. Effeminacy, on the contrary, equalled free-spending (an interesting ambiguity), debt and decay. Love's loss was indeed Empire's gain.

Similar assumptions often permeate the thought of the self-consciously masculine in our own day; the novelist Ernest Hemingway, for instance. Both in his writings and in his private life he made much of his manly virtues: toughness, bravery, dedication. A curious creature, he caricatured the virtues he actually possessed: a man, brave in battle, who invented stories about being brave in battle; a man of great physical prowess who bragged unconvincingly about his strength and toughness. Like William Acton, he believed in the complete differentiation of men from women; and he also shared Acton's quasi-economic view, that man has only a limited supply of sexual energy, and that what he spends now he cannot spend later. Also, and even more illuminating, he believed that sexual indulgence undermined the discipline of writing: that writing, fighting and sexuality all sprang from a common psychic source.[4]

Argument by historical and literary example is too easy, though. It is probably an error to make too much of this Victorian substratum in our present system of values. Long before Acton's day, the arts, and the theatre particularly, were seen as vaguely licentious; and puritans for centuries have attacked any form of display. Puritanism, in its turn, did not begin with the Reformation. Nor for that matter with St Augustine. There seem to have been powerful Manichean strains in Christian thought from the time of its earliest inception. It follows that the systems of meaning that cluster about psychology today, if not perennial, are certainly long-standing. And one of the most interesting attempts to illumin-ate them remains, in my view, Norman Brown's. I am not competent to judge at the level of systematics whether his effort to knit together Freud's thought with Marx's is a success. But it is addressed to appropriate issues, and it gives us a language with which to agree or disagree – among others, with Brown himself.

In *Life Against Death*, Brown rejects as insipid neo-Freudian dilutions of the Master's vision; and he reaffirms Freud's insist-ence on the conflict between life and death instincts, Eros and Thanatos. Brown presents Eros and Thanatos not solely as impulses or well-springs, but as a shorthand for our two modes of address to the world about us; the modes whereby we act on our surroundings, and thereby construct our sense of who we are. Eros he conceives as the impulse to have access to someone else's mind, to share their experience; Thanatos as the urge to control, to turn our knowledge into some lifeless form. Eros seeks 'to preserve and enrich life'; Thanatos, 'to return life to the peace of death'.

This opposition neatly encompasses the otherwise puzzling association that seems to lurk at the back of our minds, linking science and masculinity with the study of the inanimate. But Brown is not content simply to stitch such ideas together into patterns; instead, he uses Freud's distinction to mount his two attacks: one, general, on the current state of the civilized order; the other, more specific, on science and technology. Freud saw civilization as the highly desirable outcome of man's repression of his own libido: the action within the head, as it were, of the death instinct on the life instinct, of the forces of inhibition on those of excitation. But the sublimation necessary to historical progress leads, Brown argues, to impoverishment; to an increase in the domain of the death instinct at the expense of the life instinct – to a living death: 'Sublimation', he says, 'is a mortification of the body and a sequestration of the life of the body into dead things.' A superb sentence; and inasmuch as it applies to the shrivelled forms of life one is free to live in a bureaucracy, it is as apt as any could be. But Brown goes on to reject Freud's own unquestioning, Comtean attitude to science; one in which man is seen as passing from savagery and super-stition to science, from mindless pleasure to maturity. In its place, and more problematically, he, like Whitehead, advocates a 'non-morbid' science, 'erotic' rather than 'sadistic' in aim. Its purpose would not be mastery over nature, but union with it. Its means would be not economic but exuberant.

Schemes constructed, like Brown's, in binary terms – whether explicit, as with Eros and Thanatos; or implicit, as in scientists' use of hard and soft – are bound in practice to be too simple. On the other hand, they offer, historically, an impressive pedigree; and they are widely if not universally employed. They are also important, as Marcuse has argued, prophylactic-ally. Pathological states seem to ensue whenever one value – Progress, Science, Democracy, Power, Race, Love – is pursued to the exclusion of all others. To negate one value with its antithesis is at least to cast matters back into a state of equilib-rium. Even so, the elements of such binary schemes need not be treated as eternally fixed; still less the nature of the relation between them. Within the universities, our assumptions about scholarship and research have changed radically in the last fifty years – great tracts of territory have been colonized for Science. My impression is that these assumptions are changing again, quite rapidly, and of their own accord. Science is no longer accepted uncritically as the expression of Progress, as the cutting edge of our civilization's fight with ignorance. Its pursuit is seen as dangerous, even lethal – and its devotees are suspected, not entirely unfairly, of substituting one system of superstition for another. Our problem, perhaps, is that the age of scientific colonialism is drawing to a close, and that – as psychologists – we must learn to live in the age of self-rule.

The Question of Indoctrination 7

In the course of the last six chapters I have edged towards the view that, in any educational establishment worthy of the name, malleable youth is coerced to think in ways of which their teachers approve. If there were one kind of excellence in matters of the mind, such a process would be uncontroversial. Training a man's mind would be like training him to lift weights: it could only be done more or less well. It was just this athletic analogy that occurred to Francis Galton – a contemporary of Acton's, and the founding father of mental testing. It has remained lodged in the imaginations of mental testers ever since. Just over a hundred years ago, Galton wrote:

> Everybody who has trained himself to physical exercises discovers the extent of his muscular powers to a nicety ... So long as he is a novice, he perhaps flatters himself there is hardly an assignable limit to the education of his muscles; but the daily gain is soon discovered to diminish, and at last it vanishes altogether ... This is precisely analogous to the experience that every student has had of the working of his mental powers ... he competes in the examinations of school and college, over and over again with his fellows, and soon finds his place among them ... with all the ambition of twenty-two years of age, he leaves his University and enters a larger field of competition. The same kind of experience awaits him here ... He tries, and is tried in many things. In a few years more, unless he is incurably

blinded by self-conceit, he learns precisely of what per-
formances he is capable, and what other enterprises lie
beyond his compass ... He is no longer tormented into
hopeless efforts by the fallacious promptings of over-
weening vanity, but he limits his undertakings to matters
below the level of his reach, and finds true moral repose in
an honest conviction that he is engaged in as much good
work as his nature has rendered him capable of perform-
ing.[1]

And each of us in his proper station. The resonance here is
unambiguously that of the well-established Victorian country
house: of the master and mistress taking tea; the butler polishing
silver; the head gardener and his underlings at work among the
roses; nanny in the nursery; cook in the kitchen; and maids in
their frilly hats, giggling fecklessly. Happily for those of us
born outside the professional classes, there are more forces at
work in heaven and academic life than were dreamt of by
Francis Galton. Happily, too, we are not now as free to inter-
lard our mistaken generalities with moral innuendo. In practice,
of course, there are as many forms of intellectual excellence as
there are intellectual traditions; and there is no known way of
setting one above another. Who, after all, is in a position to
say that excellence in physics is more excellent than excellence
in history; in psychology than in, say, literary criticism? Each
discipline, each school of thought, has its own standards,
loyalties, and institutional underpinning.

The physical and biological sciences, admittedly, have
evolved their own Whig history, heaping praise, sometimes
misleadingly, on those who turned out to be on the right
track, and ignoring those who were on the wrong. But
elsewhere, clear criteria of progress are lacking, so even this is
beyond us. The lengthiest of historical perspectives will not
tell us with any satisfactory degree of certainty which historians,

painters or psychologists to include in our Pantheon, and which to omit.

This interesting state of affairs has consequences, especially where rival schools of thought exist, as they often must, within a given academic field. For where absolute standards of progress, let alone of merit, are absent, the teacher's role is bound to become more or less subtly polemic. In just the sense that the presuppositions of upper-middle-class Victorian society permeate Galton's reasoning, those of any particular school of thought are used by its teachers to permeate the minds of their students: establishing internal standards of value, aligning loyalties, governing – at the most primitive level – what is noticed and what ignored. In short, a successful academic training both focuses and restricts the meanings its students are free to perceive.

In order to focus and restrict the meaning of what is otherwise a dangerously woolly proposition, I will be autobiographical and quite specific. Walking in London one day, soon after completing my Ph.D. – to be pedantic, in Welbeck Street, on the left-hand pavement as you walk south – it occurred to me that the figures coming towards me were not walking objects, but fields or foci of perception. Just as they were elements in my perceptual field, so was I in theirs. Ontologically, we were all of the same status; we were all the same kind of thing. Welbeck Street was full, suddenly, not of clusters of flesh and bone in motion, but of sensation. A belated discovery, to be sure; but it arrived at the time with the force of revelation. A stride or two more, and it occurred to me that someone called Laing had written a book on the matter. Hurrying to the Tavistock Institute, I borrowed their copy of *The Divided Self* and read it with delight in the train from Liverpool Street back to Cambridge. The sense of revelation was heightened, incidentally, by the presence on the opposite seat of a man with one brown eye and one green.

This incident is thought by psychiatric friends to reflect poorly on my mental health. It may well be so. But it also reflects, I feel, the power of my teachers in psychology to shape even this most basic level of perception along mechanistic lines. And it is at levels as primitive as this that what we learn and what we ignore is determined.

More recently, teaching social psychology to young Cambridge anthropologists, I found in my class an exile from the Free Speech Movement at Berkeley. He had been admitted, literally, from jail. Though an uncritical devotee of phenomenology and existential psychiatry, he was one of the two ablest students I have ever taught. He was also by nature disruptive; and I had never before faced a wrecker of high intellectual quality. In seminar after seminar, we sat at opposite ends of a dusty baize table in the Department of Archaeology and Anthropology, I trying to lead the discussion into useful channels, he giggling and commenting behind his hand.

Eventually, we were on terms with one another; and at the end of the year, he wrote examination answers of a sophistication that none of his class-mates could match. Two events seemed to lead to our rapprochement. The more important was a rambling discussion we had after hours, in which I established what I think was perceived as a certain authenticity of attitude towards the works of Ronald Laing. The other exchange was briefer and more eloquent. I was giving out references for the next meeting, among them an article about recent research on the physiology of male and female brains. Outlining its contents, I had said that sex differences in brain function looked as though they were caused hormonally, before birth, as well as culturally, after birth. At this point, and for the first time, my Free Speech student came quite clean. He said, with indignation and complete clarity: 'But *no one* thinks things like that.'

His implication was twofold. That as a matter of fact all

psychological differences between the sexes are culturally determined. And that anyone who doubted this was a fascist beast. Flustered, I suggested that he read the article and consider the evidence. My surmise is that he did so, although he never admitted it. My hope is that he learnt in this instance to distinguish fact from ideology: the fact, if it proves so, that for biological reasons men's and women's brains function along different lines, being irrelevant to the rights and dignities men and women are afforded.

This transaction depressed me, and retailing it depresses me still. It demonstrates that basic conflicts of intellectual tradition are not matters of detailed interpretation or nuance. The point of such traditions, their stuff and substance, lies in their control over the simplest levels of mental functioning – what we attend to, and what we dismiss out of hand. Within traditions and disciplines, as within societies, it is possible to achieve a certain delicacy and precision. But challenge the legitimacy of either discipline or society, and the issue polarizes at once into the most elementary categories of which man is capable: us and them, clean and dirty, right and wrong.

My own university education is certainly analysable in these terms, in philosophy and psychology alike. As a student, I could not understand Sartre. Nor, had I read him, would I have understood Merleau-Ponty. Nor Lévi-Strauss. Nor can I now, except by the most strenuous effort. This rejection of the Continental tradition was the work not so much of individual teachers, but of the discipline to which they collectively belonged, the exclusiveness of the empirical tradition being implicit in the very fabric of what we were taught. Excellence was defined in terms of verbal precision; meaning was defined either in terms of public fact or of formal logic. Such a system ensures that any examination of general and imprecise ideas is viewed as bogus, or self-evidently mistaken. My philosophical training thus had the quality of a benign and

G

quite inadvertent indoctrination. Whole areas of thought, contemporary and historical, were tacitly rejected as illegitimate, unacceptable, bad. Pedagogically, two of our psychology teachers were more down to earth. I learnt because I was afraid of their scorn. Such pressure is by no means exceptional, and by no means the preserve of experimental psychologists. I have seen it used openly by disciples of the Great Tradition in the English novel; by molecular biologists who are convinced that the key to all human mysteries lies in their hands; and more openly still by politically alert sociologists.*

Even with the benefit of hindsight, I can still detect only chinks in the armour of those who taught us. In fact, only one of any importance: the fact that, as I have said, we were taught little history, little hagiography. We learnt that if we could pull a man's arguments to pieces, we had the implicit right to step into his shoes. And where other features of our training militated against change, this invited it; for the rule of intelligence is the licence whereby the young devour the old. But this loophole aside, the intellectual training I received amounted to an indoctrination. For affection, respect and fear of being bullied or rejected are all powerful agents of persuasion. If a teacher successfully transmits his own beliefs about the limits of legitimate inquiry he is, de facto, an indoctrinator. Yet it is a condition of productive brain-work that one is committed to a discipline of some sort. So, it would seem that the teacher who leaves his students' minds open, in a state of promiscuous athleticism, is scarcely a teacher at all. His proper function, in other words, must be an ambiguous one: he must

---

* Doris Lessing's complaint about her Marxist contemporaries puts the victim's point of view well: 'Yet when I look back to that group under the trees, and recreate them in my memory, suddenly I know it's nonsense. Suppose I were to meet Maryrose now, all these years later, she'd make some gesture, or turn her eyes in such a way, and there she'd be, Maryrose, and indestructible ... And so all this talk, this anti-humanist bullying, about the evaporation of the personality becomes meaningless for me at that point when I manufacture enough emotional energy inside myself to create in memory some human being I've known.'[2]

transmit an intellectual tradition with gusto, and instil loyalty to it, but leave open the possibility of gradual or even revolutionary change. And what matters in practice is not so much the teacher's motive, nor even his style, as the elbow-room he allows.*

What in retrospect is so startling about Oxford was the totality with which our mentors took command of us. This was particularly so in psychology. The brand of mechanistic, empirical psychology we were taught was perceived – by myself certainly, and I am sure I was not alone – as the latest expression of an established science: massive in scale, authentic beyond serious question. We had no hint of how recently this type of psychology had sprung up – it was, in this country, a post-Second World War, mushroom growth – nor how uncertain its institutional basis was, and until quite recently remained.

There had been a professor of psychology at Oxford for only nine years when I first went to the Institute in 1955. The Institute's position in the university was still marginal; and many of those in authority, influenced by the prejudices of more traditional philosophers, assumed that psychology was of its very nature a fraud or hoax. No breath of such precariousness reached us. I was, for example, the first scholar of my college to be allowed to read psychology, although, at the time, the oddity of this did not strike me. Had we realized what prejudice surrounded us, we would have dismissed it, I am sure, for what in many cases it was: backwoods reaction.

At Cambridge, psychology was of longer standing. Like the Oxford Institute, the Laboratory had been established largely by personal endowment. But the university there was less hostile. Zangwill was the second professor, and his

---

* In its own terms, my Oxford education deserves 'alpha', or even 'alpha plus' for its sense of excitement and intellectual energy; no more than 'beta minus', even 'beta double minus' for its willingness to countenance criticism in any but its own terms.

predecessor, Sir Frederic Bartlett, had had a long and distinguished reign. None the less, it is still less than a hundred years since the Cambridge University Senate threw out the idea of a psychophysics laboratory, on the grounds that it would 'insult religion by putting the human soul in a pair of scales'.

Our subject was not merely an administrative novelty, it also lacked intellectual roots. Ideas which I assumed stretched back into the history of man had in fact been imported to this country from America during the 1940s. As Hearnshaw points out in his history of British psychology, not one of the more authoritative British psychologists in the inter-war period was much influenced by Watson's behaviourism, and neither Bartlett nor Zangwill had had much truck with it.[3] Hearnshaw also remarks that at least half of the professors of the more influential psychology departments in the United Kingdom *after* the Second World War had been Bartlett's pupils, a fact that might tell in favour of a conspiracy theory of academic promotion, but tells against a conspiracy theory of academic fashion – unless, an unlikely thought, the conspiracy in question was one among his pupils to negate Bartlett's influence.

Of the three roots of Cambridge psychology, one lay in its connection with physiology, another with philosophy, and the third with social and industrial psychology. When he became the first lecturer in experimental psychology in 1897, W. H. R. Rivers' room was in the physiology department; and in my own time the physiology and psychology departments of the university were still neighbours in the same building. By the late 1950s, the outward signs of all three connections still remained, but the second and third had been drained of intellectual substance. Within the walls, and among the young and assertive, the science of behaviour had taken over, the embodiment of Progress: blandly optimistic, cheerfully wrapped, a little tasteless – like American bread. It was on this thin diet that we nourished ourselves. And like students anywhere, we created a hagiography of our own. Just as Chomsky refers back to Descartes, and Laing to Sartre, so the hard young men of the Cambridge Laboratory invoked the cyberneticist, Johnny von Neumann, and, symbolically perhaps, Kenneth Craik, known to us as the most brilliant young Cambridge psychologist of his generation, a man of infinite promise which he died too young to realize. But instead of hearkening back to the wisdom of their forbears, as those in more humane branches of the discipline so often do, my more acceptable contemporaries aligned themselves with the forces of enlightenment: with the banishment of superstitious, intuitive and artistic modes of thought, and the ushering in of the new technological aesthetic, in which Rational Man is King.

Shallow, Panglossian stuff this now seems, as undemanding intellectually as it was unjustified by any identifiable achievement. Its power while it lasted, its sense of inevitability, is none the less hard to overestimate. And men who believe that they are the human vehicles of a historic force must be excused if they find it natural to exercise the administrative machinery in ways that ensure the success of their cause. There is, after all, little point in giving good degrees and influential jobs to those with retrograde or historically irrelevant attitudes.

The politics of such a situation deserve more attention than they have so far received. Students who wish to question the prevailing orthodoxy tend in practice to receive poor degrees. And those who get good degrees, but still wish to question, are edged – indeed move of their own volition – towards peripheral positions in their profession. They are labelled as mavericks, and are encouraged to work outside the conventional career structure of a teaching department, or outside academic psychology altogether. Their work is usually couched in terms unacceptable to the more established professional journals; and even if it is published, it usually fails to fill a place in the curriculum, and as a consequence is not given in lists of references to students. And if, in this turbulent age, students refer to such works spontaneously, the authority of their authors is undermined as unsound.

Until recently, we were free, like Galton, to see all this in absolute terms: the best reach the top, and the second best find sociological excuses for failing to do so. This freedom has now disappeared, and we can now make such assertions only as proclamations of faith. The academic teacher in psychology is now seen as the agent of the particular tradition or *Weltanschauung* he represents; and the examinations he sets are seen as that tradition's well-honed edge. Again, let me give an example. Twice in two years now, I have known of able students who have felt themselves trapped by a particular internal examiner. Both knew that he would demand knowledge of his own recondite research; and both felt that it would be an act of intellectual dishonesty to knuckle under. One stuck to his guns, answered only those questions he believed in, and was given a Third. The other effected an uneasy compromise, and was given a Lower Second. Without well-placed friends, such young men, lacking good Seconds, would be banished from academic psychology once for all.

If the department and the examiner are hard, potential research workers in the softer areas are weeded out at source. Both department and examiner, in other words, can ensure that a radical challenge to their conception of the subject is unlikely to occur from within it. The persuasive, and if necessary the coercive, resources of such university teachers are formidable. But beneath their exercise of power there runs at least a hint of distaste, even fear. A revealing anecdote did the rounds of the Cambridge Laboratory, year after year. It concerned medical students between the world wars. They clamoured, or so the story went, for courses on the mental disorders they were going out to face in general practice. Reluctantly, the professor provided these. The joke lay in the contents of the course. The students expected Freud, Jung, Adler. What they were given was a course on the physiology of the eye and the ear. Probably distorted, perhaps apocryphal, this anecdote was repeated to me several times, by different members of the Laboratory. It seemed to afford solace, even gratification. There was danger, it was implied, in allowing students to indulge their curiosity about their own inner workings; and both security and virtue in thwarting them.

The rawest tyro of social science is now bound to ask a functional question. Simply: Why? Why has mental discipline, and in particular academic psychology, taken the shape it has? The Marxists have a ready answer. In Marcuse's view, both linguistic philosophy and experimental psychology exist to prevent students asking searching questions: about their disciplines, about society, and – specifically – about the military–industrial complex of which the university is a part. Academic discipline exists to make what is given seem normal, irrespective of how socially or morally outrageous the given may be.

The empiricist's intuitive response to such an interpretation is one of ridicule. But this is merely to grant Marcuse his point. The education I myself received undoubtedly had the effect he predicts: I was equipped neither with the language, nor the concepts, nor the self-confidence, to phrase questions of a general kind. We were taught to dismantle, but not to reconstruct; the doctrines of the philosophers acting – as Bertrand Russell has said – as a 'corrosive solvent' of the great systems of the past, yet putting nothing, beyond a mood of sceptical complacency, in their stead. But even granted all this, Marcuse's argument still smacks of over-simplification: it is too reductive, and too pat. In a fumbling way, I am now phrasing general questions, and I am far from alone in doing so. Academic orthodoxies do live long and stubborn lives; but they eventually collapse, frequently with surprising speed – not hacked down, but wafted away painlessly in a change of the prevailing *Zeitgeist*. And social processes, even those in universities, rarely in any case have the elegance of conspiracy, of a capitalist's plot.

The beginnings of a better explanation may lie in the recognition that the antipathy between soft and hard is mutual, but expressed in different terms. The hard tend to express themselves, as Galton did, morally. Take Donald Broadbent, for example, in the course of his recent attack on Chomsky:

> It seems to me inevitable that an approach to psychology through the armchair, by the exercise of fallible human reason, intuition and imagination, will lead one to such hostility and disagreement with other people. If we refuse to use experiment and observation on other human beings, we start to regard them as wicked or foolish. I think this is a serious danger, and I have no doubt whatever that the methods of empirical psychology are socially more hygienic, or to use the older and more robust phrase, morally better.[4]

'Experiment and observation on other human beings' is here proposed as a social ethic. Intuitively, and 'through the armchair', it has much to recommend it. As Thomas Sprat pointed out three hundred years ago, in writing *The History of the Royal Society of London*, the contemplation of nature 'draws our minds off from past or present misfortunes', and 'permits us to raise contrary imaginations upon it'; whereas the 'consideration of Men, and humane affairs, may affect us with a thousand various disquiets'. On the other hand, to use nothing but observation and experiment may simply ensure that experimental research continues to act as vehicle – and eventually as justification – for the experimenter's personal prejudices and needs. Such research may tell us, implicitly, a great deal about the psychologist who designs it; but as far as the people studied are concerned, we may discover nothing searching about them at all. Worse, to treat people as natural objects may prove as unhygienic, socially and psychically, as it is scientifically unefficacious.

There is, too, an assumption made by the tough-minded, and to a lesser extent by the rest of us on their behalf, that they are somehow in the right: that those who accept a particular intellectual discipline are, in some subtle respect, legitimate, whereas those who do not are freebooters, or dilettantes. Within psychology, the experimental and self-consciously scientific argue from the stance of the established; the more speculative and humane are cast, indeed cast themselves, in the role of outsiders. Legitimacy and intellectual discipline are thus linked; and this linkage is, as Freudians would say, over-determined.

Several lines of argument converge here. First, there is the authority of Science that the more scientific psychologists feel free to borrow – though why this should carry more weight than reference to humane virtues, I do not quite see. Second, there is the general semantic connection, mentioned in the last chapter, that links together ideas of emotional restraint, toughness and social value. Third, and more diffusely, there is the cultural connection between masculinity and authority, both domestic and social. Fourth, the possibility raised by Mary Douglas that maintenance of boundaries and the use of systems of classification is inherently, structurally, related to ideas of purity and virtue.[5] Lastly, within psychology, it seems that a certain authority is assumed in the very nature of the explanation that the scientific psychologist advances. He posits laws in which the individual's self-awareness plays no part, either as evidence, or as a component of the laws themselves. He explains the individual in exactly the same way that he might explain volcanic eruptions, bird migration, or cancer. The more humane psychologist, on the other hand, constructs at least part of his explanation of a person's life in terms of the reality that that person perceives. Implicitly, he grants that individual's judgment a validity which the behaviourist denies. And to grant validity in this way is to abdicate the authority which possession of some higher knowledge imparts.

The issue may also have overtones of inverted social snobbery. In most British universities, scholars in the arts often give themselves airs of gentility that among scientists are rare. The stance of the scientific psychologist may thus have about it something of the air of the self-made man: a compound of self-confidence and rigidity that overlays a more subterranean sense of not belonging. He defends the scientific method with just the clarity of purpose that the businessman defends private enterprise: both are faiths that their owners cannot afford to have shaken. And although, like the businessman, he sometimes aspires to liberal pursuits, to the study for instance of 'creativity', he only does so on his own reductive, assimilative terms. On this view, the softer tend to react to their harder neighbours as waning gentlefolk react to those who persist in building bungalows on good arable land: with ineffectual disdain.

And if the tough-minded tend to moralize at us, the tender are more often defensive, occasionally even paranoid. My Free Speech student certainly saw the phenomenological tradition in psychology as an assertion of human individuality, and conventional social and academic discipline as its enemy. Both Laing and Jules Henry make a similar point. Here Laing expounds Henry's view, approvingly:

It is Henry's contention that education in practice has never been an instrument to free the mind and the spirit of man, but to bind them ... Children do not give up their innate imagination, curiosity, dreaminess easily. You have to love them to get them to do that. Love is the path through permissiveness to discipline: and through discipline, only too often, to betrayal of self. What school must do is to induce children to want to think the way school wants them to think.[6]

This assumption of hostility on the part of teachers, the agents of academic discipline, to the antic component in human life is expressed eloquently by the poet David Black:

In their
limousines the
teachers come: by
hundreds. O the
square is
blackened with dark suits, with grave
scholastic faces. They
wait to be summoned.
                    These are the
educators, the
father-figures. O you could
warm with love for the firm lips, the
responsible foreheads. Their
ties are strongly set, between their collars. They
pass with dignity the exasperation of waiting.

A
bell rings. They turn. On the
wide steps my
dwarf is standing, both hands raised. He
cackles with laughter. Welcome, he cries, welcome
to our elaborate Palace. It is indeed. He
is tumbling in cartwheels over the steps. The
teachers turn to each other their grave faces.

With
a single grab they have him up by the shoulders. They
dismantle him. Limbs, O
Limbs and delicate organs, limbs and
guts, eyes, the tongue, the
lobes of the brain, glands; tonsils, several
eyes, limbs, the tongue,
a kidney, pants, livers, more
kidneys, limbs, the tongue
pass from hand to hand, in their serious hands. He is
utterly gone. Wide
crumbling steps.

They
return to their cars. They
drive off smoothly, without disorder;
watching the road.[7]

Such distaste for mental discipline is intelligible to most of
us, and it is not without factual support.* It should give us
pause, I feel, when men who have changed the face of the
earth claim, as they often do, that they found their school-
rooms and university lecture-halls places of intolerable constraint:

> ... after I passed the final examination, I found the con-
> sideration of any scientific problems distasteful for an
> entire year ... It is in fact nothing short of a miracle that the
> modern methods of instruction have not yet entirely
> strangled the holy curiosity of enquiry; for this delicate
> little plant, aside from stimulation, stands mainly in need

---

* MacKinnon, for example, reports that many of his famous men and women found
school antipathetic; both Getzels and Jackson, and Kogan and Wallach report that
teachers prefer teaching students of convergent rather than divergent temperament.[8]

of freedom; without this it goes to wreck and ruin without fail.

They had no sympathy with youth; their one object was to stuff our brains and turn us into erudite apes like themselves. If any pupil showed the slightest trace of originality, they persecuted him relentlessly, and the only model pupils whom I have ever known have all been failures in later-life.

But it should also give us pause that while the first of these familiar quotations is from Einstein,[9] the second is from Hitler's table-talk.[10] Between them, they suggest a limitation of the libertarian view: that it is a mistake to equate freedom with the maximization of human talent, either at the level of the individual, or at that of nations.*

In Laing's work especially, the increasingly direct perception of the malign streak in the civilizing process that educational systems perform seems to verge on the Rousseauesque. He hints at a Golden Age. Yet it cannot be that simple. Any cultural or intellectual system constrains; and it is precisely through systems of social and intellectual organization – family, school, university, laboratory; the arts, philosophy, science – that creativeness finds its expression. No constraining structure, no creativeness: only mouthings. Like Hobbes's 'man in a state of nature', we are at a loss without cultural systems to lend our ideas shape and meaning; systems which, if the time is ripe and the ability ours, we can elaborate, modify, or occasionally – like Einstein or Hitler – overturn.

---

* Both Laing and Black are Scots; and Scottish education is in certain respects as oppressive of human flamboyance as any in the world. The spirit of John Knox, that arch enemy of the antic, still stalks the aisles of the Scottish primary school. Only there, in the whole civilized world, do grown men still beat small girls on the hand with a leather strap for failures to learn. Perhaps it is this that has led Laing to underplay the obscenity that freedom can permit.

The tough-minded try to persuade us that they have privileged access to the moral order; the tender condemn the violence that orderly life does to the human psyche. The conflict is one that cries out for a synthesizing stride; for a more subtle conception than we yet possess of the relation between discipline and the creative impulse. The empirical tradition, unfortunately, is not one in which notions of antithesis, tension and paradox play much part. Its adherents are taught to think more monolithically; to grind at apparent contradictions until these are reduced to a homogeneous paste. The possibility that incongruity or inconsistency can act as a source of vitality does not spring naturally to the empirical mind. Yet it is some such model that students of the human order now seem to me to need. And they need it not merely in coming to terms with their subject-matter; but in making sense of the body of thought they themselves produce.

False Science

8

The hegemony of the hard-nosed within psychology, and the mutual hostilities consequent upon it, have had unfortunate consequences which I now wish to exemplify. The discipline's health is suspect: as Zangwill remarked, it has failed to produce a coherent body of scientific law; and its fruits, unmistakably, have about them an air of triviality. Attempts to justify psychological research in terms of its social utility at present lead inexorably to bathos. There is little that we have produced in the last fifty years that is, in any sense of that complex word, 'relevant': the Eleven-plus examination, behaviour therapy, motivational research for advertising, automatic landing devices for aircraft – the list is short, and, to say the least, ideologically fragile. One might as well try to justify space exploration in terms of its technological 'spin-off', the non-stick frying-pan. Pursuit of the 'great god Science' has not only generated faulty recipes for the conduct of psychological experiments, it has come to express a philosophy of life. And this in its turn has drawn psychologists, unwittingly, into the realm of polemic.

My first intimation of the polemical possibilities of psychology concerned an issue we are now bored with, for the time being at least: the interview. The late 1940s and early 1950s were a period in British psychology when the tough-minded laid siege to their more clinical, tender-minded brethren. The interview was at stake, because, like psychoanalysis, it was a form of human appraisal based essentially on intuition. The tough-minded objection to both techniques was, simply, that they did not work. Eysenck put the point with characteristic vigour: 'This failure of the interview is only one of many instances showing the impossibility of achieving reliable and valid prediction on the basis of subjective ratings, personal impressions, and clinical insight ...'[1] By the time I had taken up psychology as an undergraduate, other authoritative voices had joined Eysenck's, notably Vernon's. An avid reader of Eysenck's paperbacks, I myself viewed both the interview and psychoanalysis as the epitome of intellectual self-indulgence; relics of the superstition that the new scientific order in psychology was sweeping away.

In my second year of research, and on an unfamiliar impulse, I looked up the reference in the *British Journal of Sociology* that all authorities had cited as damning the interview beyond hope of salvation; and I have never quite recovered from my surprise at what I found there. The evidence bore almost no relation to the interpretations that had been placed upon it.

All this is now behind us.* The research took place more than twenty years ago; and the misinterpretations of it began only a few years thereafter. One unguarded commentary led, apparently, to others; the misunderstanding gaining weight from every authority who repeated it. None can have checked the original source at first hand. Happily, even the terms of reference of the debate itself now seem dated. It is no longer a question of whether interviews are 'valid' or 'invalid'. Nor even a question of whether a particular kind of interview is valid or not. In all probability, some forms of interview – the Oxford viva, perhaps – will turn out more useful than others – oral examinations, let us say, given to medical students in anatomy and physiology. On the other hand, all interviews could prove useless as means of selecting or examining students,

---

* The study in question was by Himmelweit and Summerfield at the London School of Economics. They, incidentally, made no untoward claim for the evidence they had collected.[2]

recruiting industrial managers, vetting professors of psychology; yet remain indispensable. They may have a stabilizing function in our paperbound society, lending a necessary, symbolic semblance of humanity to processes that are in truth bureaucratic. We are still almost as ignorant about such issues as we were when research on interviewing began.

The moral is not one about interviews but about psychologists. When a cultural tide begins to flow through the subject – in this case, in favour of science and rigour, and against the mystique of personal judgment – niceties of evidence and inference are overlooked. The large majority of those who overlook them do so in good faith and unawares; and among them are men who believe in the scientific method as the highest virtue. It is a field in which a determined piety offers little protection against error; indeed, the steelier the determination, the greater the chances of self-deception seem to become.

A more troubled example of this process lies in the recent debate about intelligence and race. Before the Second World War, psychology was disfigured by a dispute, now notorious, about the origins of intelligence. Some claimed that differences between individuals were largely a matter of their chromosomes and genes; others, in debt to the social sciences, argued that such differences sprang from upbringing and cultural expectation. After the war, the argument petered out. The profession seemed content to agree that the debate had been ill-conceived; and, more important, that it was not producing interesting research.

Meanwhile, the attack of the tough on the tender was diverted into less socially explosive channels: into the debate, for example, about the validity of psychoanalysis and the interview. The reason for this change of heart is plain to see. Whilst members of the hereditary and environmentalist camps pawed the ground at one another, and breathed hot air, the Western world was girding itself up for an act of unparalleled racial

H

obscenity. After Auschwitz and Belsen, the hereditary view – the belief that some of us are genetically superior to others – understandably, if temporarily, lost much of its sway.

And so the environmentalists had the field to themselves; and, quite rapidly, they ran amok. Soon, *all* differences between individuals were being explained as the result of parents' possessive violence on their children, of one man's manipulation of his neighbour's mind. The tender now laid siege on the tough; and began to reveal their own brand of aggression. It is symptomatic of our times that the backlash should come from a professor of Educational Psychology at the University of Berkeley: a place of learning that has been ruined by young men and women who have read a little sociology, and now proclaim, with passionate sincerity, the infinite plasticity of mankind.

Professor Jensen's widely publicized article in the *Harvard Education Review* was bred of exasperation; its author makes no bones about it. He fires a broadside, in favour of population genetics, and against villainous environmentalism. His thesis, in outline, is that efforts to raise children's I.Q.s, especially Negro children's I.Q.s, have failed, not, as the interested spectator might imagine, because attempts have been incompetent, but because I.Q.s cannot be raised. Largely, they are under the control of the genetic code. Both Negroes and the working class are born inferior and remain so. There are reservations and hedgings of various kinds; but this is the gist of what he has to say.

Jensen's article is in fact a review, long and biased, stretching for 123 pages. Most of the material he touches on is familiar, much of it stale. He rests heavily, for example, on the well-known studies of identical twins, apparently without realizing that they are as open to an environmentalist interpretation as they are to a genetic one. But a few of his 159 references are less well-worn; and one in particular caught my attention:

One of the most striking pieces of evidence for the genetic control of mental abilities is a chromosomal anomaly called Turner's syndrome. Normal persons have 46 chromosomes. Persons with Turner's syndrome have only 45. When their chromosomes are stained and viewed under the microscope, it is seen that the sex-chromatin is missing from one of the two chromosomes that determine the individual's sex. In normal persons this pair of chromosomes is conventionally designated XY for males and XX for females. The anomaly of Turner's syndrome is characterized as XO. These persons always have the morphologic appearance of females but are always sterile, and they show certain physical characteristics such as diminutive stature, averaging about five feet tall as adults. The interesting point about Turner's cases from our standpoint is that although their I.Q.s on most verbal tests of intelligence show a perfectly normal distribution, their performance on tests involving spatial ability or perceptual organization is abnormally low (Money, 1964). Their peculiar deficiency in spatial-perceptual ability is sometimes so severe as to be popularly characterized as 'space-form blindness'. It is also interesting that Turner's cases seem to be more or less uniformly low on spatial ability regardless of their level of performance on other tests of mental ability. These rare persons also report unusual difficulty with arithmetic and mathematics in school despite otherwise normal or superior intelligence. So here is a genetic aberration, clearly identifiable under the microscope, which has quite specific consequences on cognitive processes. Such specific intellectual deficiencies are thus entirely possible without there being any specific environmental deprivations needed to account for them.[3]

Read quickly – as quickly, one fears, as it was written – this paragraph makes a sharp impression. When one of forty-six chromosomes is missing, there exists a corresponding loss of a specific mental ability. Genetic effects this neat are not come by every day. I had not myself heard of Turner's Syndrome, and knew of Money's work only in another context. Accordingly, I sought out the university's only copy of his article and read it.[4] It would be misleading to say that Jensen's interpretation bore no relation to what Money had written: there were, throughout, resemblances. But there were also discrepancies on almost every point of substance, and these were systematic. Each one served to sharpen the case Jensen wished to make.

Take first Turner's Syndrome itself. As Money describes it, this is a clinical condition in which women's ovaries are rudimentary or missing, and in which both menstruation and normal sexual development fail to take place. Sufferers are also somewhat dwarfed. Some of them, too, have gross physical defects: webbed neck, shield-like chest, abnormal porousness of the bones, deformed nails. The pattern of symptoms, in other words, is somewhat loose-knit. And already there is a divergence between Money's evidence and Jensen's account of it. He acknowledges these women's sterility, but fails to mention their more general lack of normal sexual development, and also their physical deformities. Both points are vital from the explanatory point of view, because the social environment of such women is bound to differ from that of women who are physically and sexually normal. They will be treated differently by men; and probably by women too.

Next, the genetic details. Again, there are major omissions. Jensen asserts that women with Turner's Syndrome have only forty-five chromosomes; the anomaly being designated 45XO, the sex-chromatin being negative. One does not need to be a geneticist to see that the story Money tells is more complicated:

The cytogenetic peculiarity most common in Turner's syndrome is a missing chromosome, so that the count is 45XO. The sex-chromatin is negative, that is to say, missing from the cells when they are test-stained. There are also cases in which the sex-chromatin is positive. The majority, if not all of these cases, have a chromosomal mosaicism.[5]

Looking at Table 1 in Money's article, one finds in fact that a third of his cases are chromatin-positive, and involve mosaics of various kinds. Four cases, for example, combine the pattern of 45XO with that of 46XX; three more combine 45XO with 46XX and 47XXX. Genetically speaking, in other words, the sample is something of a hotch-potch.

Next, the number of cases involved. In all, Money deals with thirty-eight cases of Turner's Syndrome. One, a gross mental defective, could do none of the tests and was excluded from his calculations. Of the original thirty-eight, only fifteen provided enough genetic information to bear on Jensen's argument; and of these fifteen, only four in fact conformed to the pattern 45XO. (In nineteen cases there is no record of a chromosome count, and in four more no record of whether the chromatin is positive or negative.) Jensen thus rests a generalization which has implications for the intelligence of the working classes of all nations, the intelligence of all Negroes as opposed to all white people, on a tiny sample of physically deformed, sterile women and girls. Giving him the benefit of various doubts, we could allow him a sample of thirty-seven. If we are to be precise, without being pedantic, he has only fifteen. Being as strict as he is with research he does not like, he has a sample of just four.

Next, the ages of Money's sample. Tacitly, Jensen gives the impression that this consists of adults. In fact, ages range from five to twenty-nine. Their scores are 'age-corrected' – a desperate statistical expedient, although, admittedly, one that clinical testers are frequently forced to employ – and thereafter small children and grown women are treated as one.

Next, the tests used. Money's evidence was accumulated, of necessity, over a period of years, using three different intelligence tests. Scores on all three are lumped together without reservation; a technical blemish, to say the least, but again one on which Jensen makes no comment.

Next, the evidence about 'space-form blindness'. Jensen makes two points here. First, he claims that while sufferers from Turner's Syndrome show normal levels of verbal intelligence, their ability with shapes and patterns is abnormally low. Second, that their ability with shapes and patterns is more or less *uniformly* low, regardless of how good they are with words. Looking at Money's data, there is no doubt that the verbal scores are on the whole higher than the scores for shapes and patterns. Even so, there are discrepancies and omissions. What Jensen does not report is that in five cases out of thirty-seven, the woman's score on shapes and patterns is actually *higher* than her verbal score, and in as many more cases the difference is negligible. And what neither Money nor Jensen mentions is that a certain weakness in dealing with shapes and patterns is normal among samples of women anyway.

Making his second point, Jensen actually contradicts the evidence rather than over-simplifying it, although Money himself is to some extent to blame here. Money's evidence shows that the higher the individual's verbal score, the more likely she is to have a presentable score with shapes and patterns. Of the eighteen whose verbal scores are average or above average for the sample, no less than fifteen had spatial reasoning scores that are also above average – a closer relation between verbal and spatial scores than one would expect to find among perfectly normal women. In short, Jensen's interpretation suggests a specific, clearly-defined gap in the individual's mental powers;

the evidence displays only tendencies, and tendencies with important individual exceptions.

Finally, one last significant omission. Jensen glosses over the fact that most sufferers from Turner's Syndrome are weak not only with shapes and patterns, but in those parts of the intelligence tests used to measure 'freedom from distractibility'. This not only blurs still more the impression that Jensen is striving to create; it also points to a radically different explanation. 'Freedom from distractibility' is based on tests of number. It follows, whatever interpretation we put upon it, that conceptual weaknesses among women with Turner's Syndrome are diffuse rather than local. They cover the whole non-verbal sphere. As both Jensen and Money suggest, this weakness could arise from an innate lack of ability. Equally, though, it could spring from an inability or reluctance to concentrate on numbers, shapes and patterns. It may be a question, in other words, not of ability, but of attitude. On the evidence, we have no means of telling.

What then does this 'striking piece of evidence' boil down to? Nothing much. To a tiny group of women and small girls, bodily and sexually deformed in various degrees. Most but not all of them show signs of a diffuse intellectual weakness in just those types of reasoning in which women are usually below par anyway. It is an intriguing piece of research, but one that is too ramshackle to demand interpretation. A genetic explanation, of course, remains entirely feasible. Mental weaknesses of this kind could well be caused more or less directly by genetic defects. Equally feasibly, they may prove to have no direct connection with genetic abnormalities at all.

Consider for a moment the possibilities. These women are manifestly odd, physically and hormonally. Women generally show a weakness in non-verbal reasoning. And skill in non-verbal reasoning is itself influenced by a child's cultural expectations: in boys, for instance, by the presence or absence of a father in the home to act as a role model. The gross physical peculiarities suffered by these unfortunate women will almost certainly influence both their own social behaviour, especially towards men, and the expectations of others – again, especially men – towards them. These unusual expectations could well in their turn undermine the girl's ability to think in a style in which most women are in any case shaky. Indeed, it may well be that all women who suffer malfunction of the sex glands – or, for that matter, any other form of physical defect that disrupts their ability to act as normal women – will show special weakness in the non-verbal sphere. No one has ever looked. We do not know.

So much for one of Jensen's 159 references. It is not that such work should be dismissed, though it is fragile enough in all conscience. Money's work is a useful, preliminary contribution to a field of knowledge just beginning to establish itself: the study of the interaction of biological and social factors in determining how we think. Of more immediate importance to us is Jensen's haste in assimilating such material to his theme. The burden of his argument is, as I have said, to deny any realistic basis for the notion of human equality. Some of us, he tells us, are born, live and die more richly endowed than others. Such assertions have an obvious polemic value: they are the stuff of racist propaganda. They have also made Jensen himself famous, someone of whom most of us have now heard. Yet one of the oddities of the situation is that Jensen himself is not a racist, nor even simply a publicist. If, in this instance, he could be said, vulgarly, to have cooked the books, he has done so in good faith; and he continues to see himself as an honest man in a nest of thieves. Studies of race and intelligence are important, he argues, not simply because the truth is important, but because this particular aspect of the truth has vital social and educational implications.

Yet in common with much evidence that looks vaguely important, Jensen's is devoid of practical relevance. Even if the ability to do tests and examinations were demonstrably under genetic control – a demonstration it is at present hard to conceive – it would still not follow, as Jensen both seems to imply and yet hotly denies, that blacks and whites should be placed in separate educational streams. Nor does it follow that any one child's ability to benefit from teaching has a fixed limit. Genetics, after all, describes only the raw material on which a particular culture acts. As educational systems evolve, so too do the skills of the individuals within them. Logically, we can set limits to children's capacity to learn only if every permutation of their environment, every method of nurturing and teaching them, has been exhausted. This is a task we have scarcely begun; and which, even in principle, we could never finish.

The modification of cultural environments and methods of teaching are, each of them, vast enterprises; and vastly more important, both scientifically and socially, than the some-what pedantic, genetic point they are at present being used to subserve. We could not test genetic claims about the I.Q.s of blacks and whites unless we were prepared to separate identical black twins at birth, and bring up one of each pair among people who did not notice that he was black. This would mean either skin bleaching, hair straightening, and some facial sur-gery, or the discovery of a society in which racial prejudice is absent. And this last would be a discovery so revolutionary, and so benign, as to render quibbles over a few points in I.Q. quite trivial.

One is forced to conclude, in the case of intelligence and race, that the question of social and educational implication is a façade. Authors like Jensen wish to make a statement about human equality, not primarily because they are concerned about the state of our schools; nor because the facts, if facts they are, should be duly, scientifically, recorded; but because they wish to combat humbug – to do down a world view that they are convinced is a self-indulgent sham. They want to be free to proclaim, as Galton could proclaim a hundred years ago: 'It is in the most unqualified manner that I object to pretensions of natural equality.'[6]

The barbs in Jensen's writings, as in Eysenck's, are directed not against racial minorities, but against the monstrous regiments of sociology – and the egalitarian, libertarian doctrines with which sociology is often associated. Their protest is against the assumption, fostered by much undergraduate teaching in the social sciences, that social conventions are not merely 'relative', but optional – in the sense that rational men can dispense with them altogether. Implicitly, in other words, their protest is against the abandonment of conventions about sexual modesty, the use of drugs, the collapse among students of the work ethic, and the collapse, too, of authoritative relations between teachers and taught – all of these being social symptoms over which sociologists have in the past been seen to cast an indulgent eye.

One also senses in psychologists like Jensen a need to use Galton's forthright style. To cut through the sticky layers of egalitarian sentiment with which social issues are nowadays surrounded; to utter dismissively, as Galton could, from the heartland of the Empire:

> I have not cared to occupy myself much with people whose gifts are below the average, but they would be an interesting study.

> The mistakes the negroes made in their own matters were so childish, stupid, and simpleton-like, as frequently to make me ashamed of my own species.

> England has certainly got rid of a great deal of refuse through means of emigration.[7]

Arthur Jensen speaks to many of us – I hope I am not among them, but who can be sure? – who wish they were still free to talk in such terms about those people whom they dislike or they fear.

The question of style is perhaps more important here than it is normally allowed to seem. As the philosopher Stuart Hampshire points out, the sources of a personal style are often, too, the sources of 'a wilful redrawing of the distinction between appearances and reality'; both individual style and philosophical assumption deriving, usually unconsciously, from a personal need.[8] Frequently if not invariably, the style betrays the man. If read with care, Jensen's work has in this respect a good deal to yield. One finds there certain of the hallmarks of the falsely scientific posture in psychology: of scientism. One finds, for example, apparently endorsed, a view of the world as simple as any could be: 'In the actual race of life, which is not to get ahead, but to get ahead of somebody, the chief determining factor is heredity.'[9]

Also, more pervasively, a hearty philistinism. A characteristic sentence: 'This particular bugaboo seems to have loomed up largely in the imaginations of those who find such great satisfaction in the idea that "fixed intelligence" has been demolished once and for all.'[10]

One senses throughout a distaste for the frills and furbelows of human self-awareness, a zeal in cutting them away. We are the creatures, he seems to tell us, of the laws of genetics, motivation, conditioning; *any* laws that are simple in form and inexorable in their action. Our tethers are short, and our powers of self-determination an illusion. One detects, too, a craving for stability – though no one should grudge a professor from Berkeley that. It is a sentiment that expresses itself in a variety of ways: in his taste for quasi-physical laws, for instance; and the venom with which he attacks social psychologists like Rosenthal, whose work blurs the edges of the simple categories mental testers use.* He also tends, in an interesting way, to reify statistical concepts like general intelligence, treating them fallaciously, as though they were mental faculties: at one point, he even likens the general factor in intelligence-test scores to the 'Rock of Gibraltar'. He seems, too, to be something of an Anglophile. Most unusually in an American writer on intelligence, he favours English references to American ones; Spearman's views to Thurstone's. He accepts Burt's research quite uncritically, referring to him by his title – 'Sir Cyril Burt' – no less than three times within thirty pages. And even his reference to the Rock of Gibraltar – a curious image for a Californian to choose, and one which could scarcely be less appropriate to its context – might be interpreted, not entirely fancifully, as unconscious obeisance to Navy and Queen.

If my interpretation is approximately correct, and if one may be forgiven a cheap pun, Professor Jensen's impulse is to call a spade a spade. And, under the influence of this impulse, he has not merely misinterpreted evidence but also confused the purposes to which it can logically be put. One's initial reaction is that of high-minded indignation – followed quickly by a wave of fear lest you have blundered equally publicly yourself. But in the light of truths about the nature of psychology now dawning, both responses seem inadequate. Our perception of meaning in our own research is a subtle affair, related only in a complex way to fact and logic. Transgressions as blatant as those surrounding Turner's Syndrome one can still condemn in the conventional way; but more baffling are the processes of selective attention that involve all of us as soon

---

* Rosenthal and Jacobson's study *Pygmalion in the Classroom* suggests that a teacher's expectations of his pupils serves to foster or inhibit the growth of those pupils' I.Q.s.[11] Like most research that breaks new ground, theirs is technically imperfect. Jensen ignores its conceptual interest, and leaps instead at certain blemishes. One detail he describes as a 'faux pas par excellence'; risky French, and risky criticism from someone in a glasshouse throwing stones.

as we relate factual evidence to some more general interpretative theme. Jensen's article could be dismissed as lying – at least in part – outside the normal confines of scientific debate; he could be discredited as someone who has fallen from the strait ways of Science. But this, I am now convinced, would be to miss the exemplary point he unwittingly affords us. Namely, that the search for meaning in data is bound to involve all of us in distortion to greater or lesser degree. Psychology should be pictured not as a society of good men and true, harbouring the occasional malefactor, but rather, as one in which everyone is searching for sense; in which differences are largely those of temperament, tradition, allegiance and style; and in which transgression consists not so much in a clean break with professional ethics, as in an unusually high-handed, extreme or self-deceptive attempt to promote one particular view of reality at the expense of all others. On this second view, Jensen is certainly not alone, and his company may prove to be very numerous indeed.

No Scientist an Island 9

By now, I have exaggerated perhaps the tendency of psychologists to adopt hard or soft postures; and have stressed unduly the polarities of intuitive meaning that underlie their everyday work. The preoccupations of empirical and more systematic philosophers; the conflict of scientific and humane tendencies within psychology; the role of teachers as initiators into traditions of thought – all these have been portrayed in cultural rather than rational terms. When they change, or so I have implied, they do so sluggishly, stirring with the deeper currents in the society at large. Changes are more rapid, of course, closer to the surface; and on the surface itself, positively evanescent, rippling with every gust of academic fashion. But even here, it is the intuitive, somnambulistic aspects of academic life I have stressed, and its permeability to the systems of value that immerse it.

This somewhat fluid view is at odds, naturally, with the scientific psychologist's view of his own activities. He sees himself as insulated in his rationality from the messy world outside his laboratory; or rather, as related to that world only in formal, specifiable ways. He acknowledges change within his subject, but sees this as internal, if not to psychology, at least to science: springing from the accumulation of knowledge in his own field, and from cross-fertilization with that in fields belonging to neighbours. He acknowledges, too, the influence of grant-giving bodies. He takes in funds, and gives out results: results that are the objective truth as best he can discern it. If his work is misinterpreted once uttered, this is the fault of pressmen, knaves and politicians; evidence of the need for more scientific education, more scientists in high office.

My contention, self-evidently, is that this vision of psychology as an island in a sea of unreason, and of psychologists as privileged castaways, is illusory: at best premature, at worst menacing. In contrast, for instance, to physics or chemistry, logical development within psychology is usually local and short-lived; and our self-deception in this matter has rendered Jensenesque distortions of evidence not merely possible but natural. It has also made it easy for psychologists, despite their failure to achieve a cumulative scientific growth, to exert a social influence that is inadvertent, and sometimes malign.

Stirrings in the wider culture have of late been more than usually obvious; and their impact on university life substantial. Beyond question, if at present beyond our powers of explanation, the last ten years have seen a radical transformation in attitudes to authority and to authoritative knowledge. In the social and behavioural sciences especially, the young are demanding an equality of status with their teachers that a decade ago was unthinkable. Where I viewed my tutors with respect verging on awe, my own postgraduate students treat me with a cautious toleration. They glance occasionally at some of the research I do; but they judge it in their own terms, not mine. It strikes them as puzzling, too, that I am in academic authority over them, and in a position to judge their work. If I praise them, this is their due; if I criticize, no more than the exercise of my own particular brand of prejudice. They treat me, in short, as an equal. And this broad change may have influenced not only students' willingness to accept their teachers' beliefs in absolute terms, but also our willingness, teachers and students alike, to countenance absolute habits of thought.

Given this new scepticism, we are now more sensitive than we were to the polemic and autobiographical sentiments lying

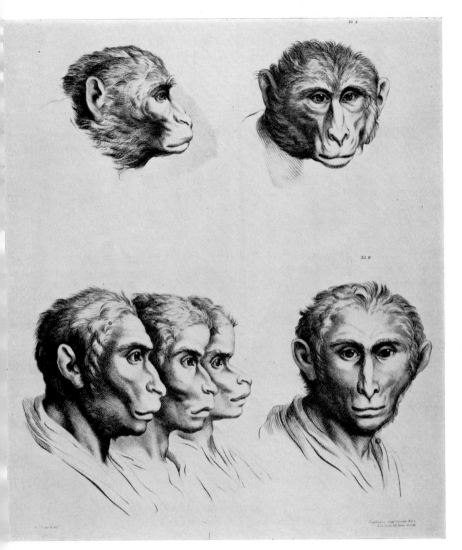

6. The behavioural metaphor, Man-as-Monkey-as-Man, by Le Brun

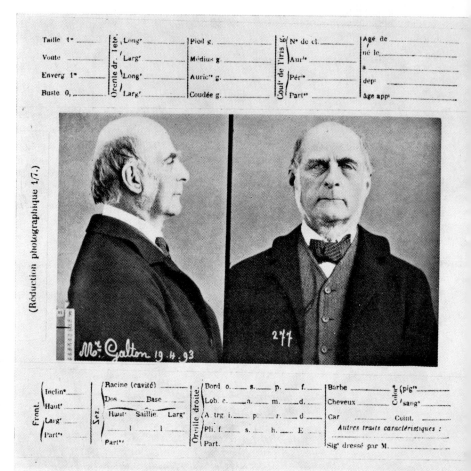

7. Francis Galton, aged 71, photographed as a criminal on his visit to Bertillon's Criminal Identification Laboratory in Paris, 1893

at the heart of work that, until recently, would have passed for the fruits of pure reason. The truth is that, to a remarkable extent, psychologists do research in their own image. One notices this daily. Psychologists with high I.Q.s do research that reflects well on those with high I.Q.s. Neurotic introverts show that neurotic introverts do well at school and university. Convergers do research that bodes well for convergers; divergers, for divergers. And those in whom, like myself, the two modes of thought conflict do research that expresses the tension between the two.* Just as novelists draw on their experience, so too do psychologists. We would both be cut off, otherwise, from the springs of our intellectual vitality. To refuse a psychologist access to his intuitions, even if this were possible, would be as stultifying and as short-sighted as it would be to deny them to a physicist or a painter. Such immediate, personal involvement becomes troublesome only when we try to conceal it; and it becomes socially dangerous only among those who feel they have some God-given licence to dictate what shape society should take. Unfortunately, it is just this sort of feeling that is widespread in the profession, and its effects can express themselves in subtle ways. It is these that I now wish to explore.

The influence of Freud on the mores of the Western world is now a journalistic commonplace. The influence of Laing, Chomsky and Marcuse on the minds of students will soon become one. Yet in each case, the nature of the influence remains a little mysterious. The somewhat harsh, patriarchal, deterministic view of human fate that Freud expressed is now associated in the popular imagination with methods of child-raising devoid of discipline or control. Rather in the same way,

---

* I was leafing the other day through a bundle of I.Q. scores gained thirty years or so ago by students and research workers in psychology, some of whom are now distinguished. In certain cases, the scores were very high indeed, in others quite low. All those with the highest scores have become mental testers, or have used mental tests in their research. None of those with low scores to my knowledge have done so.

the vogue for linguistics and for the Chomskean approach to transformational grammar has taken its own heroes somewhat by surprise. Audiences of eager students listen not to the literal content of what is said – often indigestibly technical – but to some message more hidden: to the 'deep' rather than the 'surface' structure of linguistics itself. One has the sense here not of the rational and explicit, but of shifts and ground-swells, of movements in the *Zeitgeist*, and of the philosophy of ripe time.

A profession now exists whose job it is to sense and to accelerate such changes: the men and women of the media. And a depressing though salutary experience it is to pass through their hands. They chop one's efforts into neat gobbets, each with its verbal tag; each shaped to suit the evolving tastes of a mass audience; each, like the end products of Bartlett's experiments in remembering, with good *Gestalt*, but shorn alike of detail and qualification. Our conventional response has been that the world of journalism is amoral, and that its emissaries should not be allowed inside the laboratory door. I am myself moving to another, gloomier view; and I propose to do no more than declare it. Namely, that in the social and behavioural sciences, success and fame, even a sense of social relevance, largely turn on whether or not a research worker's work can be packaged for the media in ways that appeal to the intelligent lay audience. A man's reputation depends on whether his research helps the able, influential but technically uninformed – vice-chancellors, politicians, civil servants – to make sense of ideas that changes in *Zeitgeist* and social circumstance are bringing just within their grasp.

For those of us who would like to be both scholarly and well-known, this conclusion is too painful to dwell upon. So I shall move on quickly – although to a possibility even more depressing, more sinister. To the danger that the very existence of a science of human life serves to cramp precisely what it purports to explain; and that it does so, not in any vague and general way, but quite specifically. Let me talk, once again, about the world of intelligence and intelligence testing. Regrettably, outrageously, the topic is a dreary one; or, at least, mental testers have contrived to make it seem so. But it also offers the clearest examples I have yet found of psychologists exercising their autobiographies at the world's expense.

The establishment of the Eleven-plus examination in British schools was, after all, a major administrative and educational feat. And it was initiated in a spirit of reform by men of unimpeachable probity. They themselves were in many cases highly intelligent products of the working class, and their motive was as natural as any could be: to give other members of that class a square deal. Conspicuous among those reformers was a predecessor of mine in Edinburgh, Sir Godfrey Thomson. In common with the rest of us, his judgment in academic matters flowed from who he was – his temperament, the upbringing he had received. Growing up in poverty on Tyneside, he attended the local board-school, and made his way against the stream by dint of natural talent and a fierce ambition. The integrity of the man shines from his autobiography.[1] Also his remoteness from the world we now occupy. Kindly and generous, he was none the less something of a martinet: for the 'dilatory, the verbose and the breakers of his rules' he had a 'quiver full of speedy thunderbolts and an unerring hand in casting them'. When a lecturer at Newcastle, he commanded the Officer Training Corps, and ran summer camps for boys in the Tyneside schools:

> ... I formed a close friendship with the bachelor Regimental Sergeant Major, and admired the way in which he lived among the sergeants, yet was addressed by them as 'sir', and at his early morning parade was saluted as punctiliously as any colonel.[2]

After a late midday meal there was afternoon school, an hour to tidy up notebooks and half an hour's singing local ballads. Then tea, games, a light supper, service and so to bed.[3]

His vision was honest, uncluttered with conceit, and entirely alien to permissive notions:

> ... when I was 14 or so, I think, or perhaps even older, someone, probably mother, gave me one after the other Samuel Smiles' books *Self Help*, *Character*, and others. It is unfashionable nowadays to think well of these, and 'the thing' to laugh at Smiles. But I cannot laugh at a man whose words at the time influenced me so strongly. I was ambitious, not only for myself but to please and be able to help mother, and I took his teaching very seriously to heart. The books were encouraging, for they were about men who succeeded, if not always in a worldly sense. And they were salutary, for all these men had struggled against poverty and other handicaps. I fear I am an unrepentant Victorian.[4]

Godfrey Thomson retired as recently as 1949, and his name is still respected by those who control what educational research the Scots are free to undertake. In my experience, mental testers are – like Thomson, and almost to a man – individuals of convergent temperament. For decades, one could not enter the field without a training in the more elaborate statistical techniques. Their world as a consequence became encapsulated, one in which like spoke only to like; in which, in Samuel Smiles's phrase, there was 'a place for everything, and everything in its place'. It is precisely the statistical nature of mental testing that attracts the convergent to it; and the tests they create embody the convergent virtues – accuracy and speed. They assume, too, a correct answer for every question;

and penalize any impulse towards irreverence, speculation or fantasy.

The strategy used in establishing the Eleven-plus was that of correlating children's I.Q.s with their school marks. The correlations being high, it was assumed without more ado that the innovation was valid. Yet this design ignores both the similarities in form between I.Q. test and school examination, and the fact that neither represents more than a fraction of the qualities that any sane teacher or psychologist would wish to foster. The testers' evidence, in other words, contained marked elements of circularity. The testers also ignored alternative interpretations of their own data – the social psychologist's argument, for example, that the testing situation favours the conforming, obedient child who wishes to please; or the sociologist's, that tests and examinations serve to stratify children socially, creating systems of self-fulfilling prophecy, without necessarily measuring children's native gifts.

The pioneers were thus doubly selective. They selected evidence, unwittingly, to vindicate their own innovation. They also, through the Eleven-plus, selected in favour of boys and girls who resembled themselves. Both are human enough failings; and neither is the preserve of mental testers. But there remains one feature of this episode that is more lingeringly disquieting: its element of conscious manipulation.

There are few British experts in this field I have not met – and almost all of them have struck me as by disposition generous. None the less, I have heard a number express, in private, violent antipathy about people of extroverted or divergent temperament. Implicitly, they take the convergent skills to epitomize all that is morally, personally and educationally desirable. The educational process that the mental testers established thus systematically penalized the kind of child they especially disliked; and it did so in a number of ways, not all immediately apparent. First and obviously, certain types of children fail the

Eleven-plus examination, and are excluded from educational opportunity. Second, they are failed by a technique that is thought to be scientific, and tend, as a consequence, to be viewed as inferior in their essence to those who pass. Third, by its very existence, the Eleven-plus helps to determine the nature of the teaching – syllabus-bound, convergent, fragmented – that potential candidates receive. And lastly, more generally, the examination serves to legitimate certain mental skills at the expense of others: again, the convergent and fragmented, at the expense of the divergent, imaginative and more rambling.

The introduction of the Eleven-plus was, evidently, an exercise in implicit ideology; in the promotion of one world view at the expense of others. To say this ten years ago would have been extreme. Now, even the most orthodox are finding ways of admitting that it is true. We now accept that when middle class give intelligence tests to working class, when white give them to black, the endeavour is cross-cultural. And more is at stake than the meanings of the words in the test. There are the meanings, too, that tester, testee, and the rest of us, read into the results.

At this point, we might step in a number of directions; though only one, I shall argue, makes sense. We could claim that the influence exerted by mental testers through the Eleven-plus was unfortunate, and hence that psychologists should hold aloof from worldly affairs. Or, we could accept involvement whole-hoggingly, and see the psychologist merely as one occupant of the arena, using his expertise as a political weapon. Or, in my view correctly, we could follow the example of Heisenberg and the physicists: retain our concern for truth, but accept that even the most disinterested attempts to measure the natural world are bound to alter it – that, in our case, the assessments we attempt of other people may influence them in profound and harmful ways. If we grant this, it follows – again, in Heisenberg's footsteps – that a knowledge of such influence and the uncertainty it entails must become integral parts of our discipline. The outpourings of psychology and social science departments, duly filtered by the media, now form part of the fluid in which our subject-matter floats. So it is not simply a matter of social morality but one of rigour that we should proceed with circumspection.

The influence of the measurer on the measured may be direct, as in the Eleven-plus. Or diffuse, through the influence of publications (about race and intelligence, for example) on assumptions prevailing in the culture at large. In either case, there are certain aspects of human life which seem especially vulnerable. Perhaps the most vulnerable of all is one on which the bearing of intelligence testing is only indirect: privacy. And the dangers present themselves most vividly in sex research, a more recent and more bizarre manifestation of man's urge to know. It provides, in fact, something of a test case for the old-fashioned, scientistic approach, and is worth examining with a little care.

Despite the pioneering efforts of the worthy and cranky, Western civilization reached the mid-point of the twentieth century knowing almost nothing about sex in a systematic way. Myths and fantasies abounded: and, as we have seen, grown men can still be found who believe, as the Victorians believed, that sexual excess leads to health and sanity impaired. Kinsey, a crank of a kind, then published his voluminous statistics about who did what, how often, when, and with whom. His collaborator, Pomeroy, describes Kinsey as the product of a strict religious background, one of the first American Eagle Scouts. He never 'dated', and married the first girl with whom he 'went steady'; their honeymoon was a camping trip. His attitudes to sex were naive:

One of his friends had come to him during Kinsey's college days, deeply worried about a sexual problem:

masturbation. The friend was so upset that he felt he had to seek advice from someone. Kinsey was shocked, but according to his upbringing knew exactly what to do. At his suggestion, the two young men knelt down in the college dormitory and together prayed that the friend be given strength to stop his masturbation.[5]

Kinsey's scientific reputation was based on field studies of the gall wasp. Over a period of twenty years or so, he collected between two and four million of them. His statistics about human sexuality have an analogous quality. What significance they possess they draw largely from the fear with which their topic is surrounded. He catalogues 'outlets' as he catalogued wasps; the quality of repetition, incidentally, having much in common with the pornographic tradition in literature, in which cataloguing and repetition are crucial constituents. He worked through interviews, but reluctantly. As Pomeroy remarks:

> ... one of the things that irked him most in later years was the fact that our sexual mores and taboos made it so much more difficult to observe human sexual responses than other natural phenomena. Yet, as we shall see, he did not allow such difficulties to stand in the way of his work. In later years Dr. Kinsey probably observed directly more human sexual responses than any other scientist – except Dr. Masters and Mrs. Johnson.[6]

It was the self-same Dr Masters and Mrs Johnson who took up the banner of sexual enlightenment where Kinsey reluctantly laid it down. They found to their surprise that the good people of St Louis were happy, in the name of Science, to perform all sorts of sexual deeds before them, in a place half operating theatre, half film studio. Again, the insights gained have been relatively sparse. But to enable volunteers to masturbate for

Science, and to do so in front of cameras and camera crew, in an atmosphere of complete legitimacy, is to alter not only those volunteers' sense of what sex means, but to alter a whole society's. What was private and personal has become more public and more impersonal. To say this is not to make a value judgment at Masters and Johnson's expense, nor to take prudish exception to the pleasure such research has doubtless afforded. Nor is it to suggest that the participants' sexual lives may not be 'happier' after the experience than before. But it is to say that Masters and Johnson have altered the nature of what they set out to observe.

Like the mental testers, Masters and Johnson have contributed to the processes of social change, protesting as they do so their unswerving allegiance to the cause of Science. One's objection, finally, is not to their involvement in change; nor even to the nature of such change, although here there are grave reservations. It is to self-deception. If the scientist is engaged in altering the values of society, intentionally or coincidentally, he should know it and say so. And such involvement should be transmitted not in laboratory gossip, but as a central and explicit part of the scientist's professional skill. The 'interpenetration of observer and observed' will then be seen not as an accident, peripheral to the social and behavioural sciences, but as the medium through which they work.

Several years ago, my brother lived for three months with an African hunting tribe, in company with an anthropologist, the anthropologist's wife, and a friend. His intention, indeed his achievement, was to make a film of the tribe. Economically primitive, the tribesmen lived by hunting game and gathering berries and fruit. Quickly, though, they realized that their visitors' rifles offered a labour-saving source of food. The point was put. The visitors quite reasonably declined, seeing this as a disruption of the tribe's ecology. In the weeks that followed, the visitors found themselves more than once in situations where they were virtually obliged to kill animals in self-defence. The tribe's stratagem culminated in an alarming vignette: my brother on one side of a clearing, an angry rhinoceros on the other. An ardent preservationist, my brother was now, almost literally, on the horns of a dilemma. To kill a rhinoceros without licence was a major transgression. Not to kill it was to run the lively risk of being impaled. To attempt to kill it and fail would only make impalement more nearly certain. In the event, luck and the instinct of self-preservation gave my brother good aim; and the rhinoceros dropped dead. The interpenetration of the social scientist and his subject-matter was thus consummated with an elegance on which Lévi-Strauss could scarcely improve. My brother reported his felony to the appropriate authority; the tribesmen cut up the rhinoceros and ate it. The scene has the economy of myth, yet it did not find its way, even as a footnote, into a published record.

Meanings and Actions 10

I have taken the view that scientific psychology has become a species of shadow-boxing. I have also assumed that the world of our thoughts and deeds is, approximately, as certain of the more perceptive novelists, poets and humane psychologists have described it. I want now to make two points: one negative, the other more open-ended. To show, negatively, that a strictly behaviouristic account of human lives is an impossibility, a fraud. And, more positively, to imply that there remains scope nevertheless for forms of inquiry into human affairs that are both systematic and 'relevant'; relevant, that is, to the world as it is, rather than as it exists in the imaginings of behavioural psychologists.

Let us take a slice of life, or rather of life-like art, and see how a psychologist might come systematically to grips with it. Michael Frayn's novel, for instance, about three Cambridge graduates in the world of journalism, *Towards the End of the Morning*. The three, in descending order of age, are John Dyson, frantic but ineffectual; the sweet-eating, talented, spineless Bob Bell; and the all-competent Erskine Morris. In the scene that follows, Dyson has appeared on television, and in the eyes of Jannie, his wife, and also of Bob, has made a fool of himself:

Dyson walked up and down the bedroom in his overcoat, making large gestures, and trailing in his wake the cosy smell of digested alcohol. Jannie lay in bed, looking at him over the edge of the covers. It was after midnight.

'Honestly, Jannie,' said Dyson excitedly, 'I astonished myself! I simply didn't know I had it in me! How did it look?'

'Very good, John.'

'Really? You're not just saying that?'

'No, John.'

'I actually *enjoyed* it, Jannie, that was the thing. I was amazed! The others were all shaking with nerves! Even hardened television performers like Norman and Frank. But honestly, I could have gone on all night. I didn't use my notes at all.'

'I thought you didn't.'

'Didn't touch them – didn't even think about them. I was absolutely in my element! How did I come over, Jannie?'

'I told you – very well.'

'I didn't cut in and argue too much?'

'I don't think so.'

'I thought perhaps I was overdoing the controversy a bit?'

'No, no.'

Dyson stopped and gazed at Jannie seriously.

'I feel I've at last found what I really want to do in life, Jannie,' he said. 'It's so much more alive and vital than journalism. Honestly, Jannie, I'm so exhilarated … !'

He began to stride up and down the room again, smiling at himself. He glanced in the mirror as he passed it and straightened his glasses.

'What did Bob think?' he asked. 'Did he think I was all right?'

'He thought you were fine.'

Dyson stopped again, smiling reflectively.

'Frank Boddy is an absolute poppet,' he said warmly. 'He really is. Oh, Jannie, I adore television! I can't tell you … ! You really think I looked all right?'

Later, as he was crawling about the floor in his under-clothes, looking under the bed for his slippers, Jannie asked:

'Why were you smoking, John?'

He straightened up and gazed anxiously over the end of the bed at her.

'You thought it looked odd?' he said.

'No, no.'

'You don't think it seemed rather mannered?'

'Of course not, John. I just wondered how you came to think of it.'

Dyson smiled with pleasure as he remembered.

'It was sheer inspiration on the spur of the moment,' he said. 'I just saw the box of cigarettes lying there on the table, and everybody else smoking, and I just knew inside me with absolute certainty that I should smoke, too. I think it absolutely *made* my performance.'

He fell asleep almost as soon as the light was out, and woke up again about an hour later, his mouth parching, his whole being troubled with a great sense of unease. What was occupying his mind, as vividly as if it was even now taking place, was the moment when he had said, 'That is absolutely fascinating, Norman,' and then realised it was supposed to be the end of the programme. Had he *really* done that? How terrible. How absolutely terrible.

He sat up and drank some water. Still, one little slip in an otherwise faultless performance... Then with great clarity and anguish he remembered the moment when Wester-man had put his question about a moral lead from the Press, and instead of answering at once the idea had come to him of leaning forward and judiciously stubbing out his cigarette. It had been scarcely a quarter smoked! He lay down in bed again slowly and unhappily.

All the same, when he had finished stubbing the cigarette

out he had given a very shrewd and pertinent answer ...
No, he hadn't! He'd taken another cigarette! In absolute
silence, in full view of the whole population of Britain,
he had stubbed out a quarter-smoked cigarette and lit a
fresh one!

He turned on to his right side, then he turned on to his
left, wracked with the shamefulness of the memory. It was
strange; everything he had done on the programme had
seemed at the time to be imbued with an exact sense of
logic and purposiveness, but now that he looked back on
it, all the logical connections had disappeared, like secret
writing when the special lamp is taken away.

And what about the time he had interrupted Lord
Boddy, and then realised that all he had wanted to say was
that it was interesting? *Extraordinarily* interesting ... Had
he *really* said that? He himself? The occupant of the tense
body now lying obscurely and privately in the dark bedroom of a crumbling Victorian house in Spadina Road,
S.W.23? Was that slightly pooped gentleman with the
waving arms who had (oh God!) told Lord Boddy that his
views were absolutely fascinating, and (oh God oh God!)
lit another of the television company's cigarettes with their
silver butane table-lighter every time he had seen the red
light come up on the camera pointing at him – was that
exuberantly shameful figure really identical with the
anguished mortal man who now lay here stretched as taut
as a piano-string in the dark?

'Jannie,' he groaned. 'Are you awake, Jannie?'

There was no reply. He turned on to his right side. He
turned back on to his left. He hurled himself on to his face.
Still Westerman and Boddy and Williamson and Miss
Drax sat around in conversation with him. He went
through his whole performance second by second, from
the moment Westerman had introduced him and he had

waved at the camera, to the moment Westerman had summed up, and he had told him it was *absolutely fascinating*. He went through it again and again, trying to improve it slightly in his memory, in the face of an increasingly hostile reception from the other four. By the time morning came he was convinced he had been wide awake the whole night, though by that time he had remembered with the utmost clarity that the whole performance had taken place not in a television studio at all, but in an enormous public lavatory, with Sir William and Lady Paice among the large crowd around the coffee table, and that his final humiliation was to discover at the end of the programme that he had been sitting on one of the lavatory seats throughout, with his trousers down around his ankles.[1]

The next morning, Dyson plunges out of his office to face the public in Fleet Street; and then to face his fellow journalists in the Gates of Jerusalem:

'Anyway', said Gareth Holmroyd finally, 'how did it go, John?'

'Terrible,' said Dyson.

'He was very good,' said Bill Waddy, arriving with more drinks for people. 'He was very good indeed.'

'You saw him, did you, Bill?' said Andy Royle.

'No, I missed him, unfortunately,' said Bill Waddy. 'Old Harry Stearns told me.'

'John was very good,' said Bob, who had told old Harry Stearns that he was very good in the first place.

'You saw him, did you, Bob?' said Ted Hurwitz.

'Yes. He was very good.'

'Yes,' said Bill Waddy, 'old Harry Stearns said he was very good.'

'Yes, he was,' said Bob. 'Very good.'

'I was terrible,' said Dyson.

'You were very good, John,' said Bill Waddy. 'Old Harry Stearns told me.'

'Good for you, John,' said Pat Selig.

'What was the programme about?' asked Gareth Holmroyd.

'The colour problem,' said Dyson.

'Well, anyway,' said Gareth Holmroyd, 'I'm glad you made a good job of it.'

It rained on and off most of the afternoon. Dyson sat back in his chair watching it, yawning, his hands behind his head. He was in a rather more agreeable mood. Jannie, Bob, old Harry Stearns, Bill Waddy, Gareth Holmroyd – they could scarcely *all* be wrong.[2]

Within a week, Dyson has a reputation as a television expert on race relations, and is invited to appear again, this time on the B.B.C. The upshot is that, through a series of accidents and misunderstandings, his place is taken by the inexorable Erskine Morris.

Frayn's account is a caricature. Most people would concede, even so, that he strikes familiar chords. He observes, digests, epitomizes; and this is what the psychologist wants to do too. But the novelist's evidence remains inseparable from his own experience. Frequently, it is identifiable as his own autobiography elaborately transformed.* As a way of doing psychology, this has its snags. At Oxford, we were initiated into the joke about the introspective psychologists who, in the early years of the century, fell into furious debate over whether green was in truth a yellowish blue, or a blueish yellow. The

* Collectively, the three central figures in *Towards the End of the Morning* could be said to offer a triangular portrait, an absurdly modest one, of a figure not entirely unlike Michael Frayn himself.

8. *The Ecstasy of St Teresa*, by Bernini

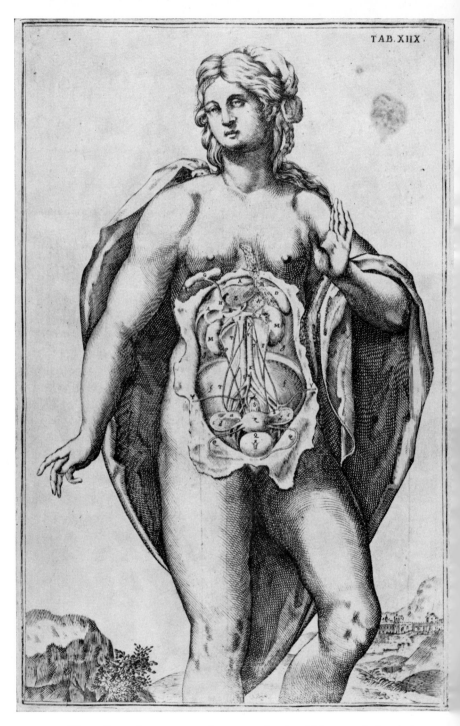

9. Venus dissected – a seventeenth-century plate in which anatomical curiosity and human respect are still combined. By J. Casserius

example is trivial, but the epistemological difficulties such a story parodies are real enough, because the science in which no two scientists can agree on the evidence is no science at all.

The behaviourists sought clarity, indeed sanity, by ignoring the realm of experience altogether. They would specify John Dyson's gesticulations towards the television cameras in the same terms as they would the actions of a rat or robot. When he said how absolutely fascinating his neighbour's views were, this would be recorded as 'vocalization'. When he remembered saying this, it could only be recorded as restlessness. Dyson's utterances, the rat's squeaks, even the robot's hum, would all be accorded an equal status. To make sense of such events, the behaviourist measures, seeks statistical regularities, makes predictions, and measures again.

The weakness of such an unselective analysis is that it does not work. The data lack any organizing principle.* As dispassionate observers, all that we could have said about Dyson that night was that his pulse rate was high, his mouth – as the author remarks – was parched, and that he slept only intermittently. If we could by some unobtrusive magic introduce the equipment of a sleep laboratory to his house in Spadina Road, we might also be able to point to disturbed patterns of electrical activity in his brain, unusual rates of eye movement, and so on. Our account rises from this bedrock of banality only by the introduction of explanatory notions culled from introspection – ideas like embarrassment, anxiety, aggression – that we can use in setting up informal models of Dyson's internal state. If the behaviourist were to relax his self-denying ordinance, he could hasten this process by asking Dyson what was on his mind. He would vocalize, in other words; and Dyson

---

* Purely behavioural analyses of rats' lives remain a remote prospect; and those whose work it is now acknowledge that such an account even of a fruit-fly's daily round is a forbidding undertaking.

K

would vocalize in return. But to make progress, he must be prepared to sin: not merely to record the noises he and Dyson make, but to interpret them as questions and answers possessing meaning. The creature who uses language, and whose language is the expression of a coherent culture, is a totally different kettle of phonemes from the creature whose vocalizations are vocalizations and nothing more.

The behaviouristic approach is either self-defeating, or it is in no real sense behaviouristic. It would be an error though to mock it for its piety. Over the next twenty-five years, we could easily lapse again into just that sterile squabbling over the meaning of evidence that behaviourism was introduced to avoid. And recent phenomenological studies – Laing's work on family interaction, for example – gain much of their point from the behavioural tradition against which they are set. To show that behaviouristic studies of family interaction are fumble-fisted is one thing; to demonstrate that one pheno-menological account of a particular family is superior to an-other is altogether more taxing. At the moment, with the behaviouristic tradition losing its original momentum, the pickings for phenomenologists are easy. They will not remain so.

Before abandoning Ur-behaviourism, we should note, and try to preserve, its compensating virtues. The observer who observes dispassionately may notice regularities that we miss in paying exclusive attention to Dyson's account of what Dyson is doing. His periods of self-doubt may be tied to his intake of alcohol; his alcohol intake, to tension between him-self and his wife; and tension between them, to the latter's menstrual cycle. Rows, among the middle class more gener-ally, may be most frequent at weekends, and be most severe for those whose working life is competitive. Dyson may be unaware of these connections, and knowledge of them may enable the psychologist to offer a better explanation than

Dyson could offer for himself. In practice, we can neither neglect Dyson's account, nor take it at its face value.

But for too long, we have taken the novelist's portrayal of Dyson on its own terms. The only person the average psychologist will ever witness burying his face in a pillow after a television performance is himself. Frayn, like all novelists and poets, enjoys privileged access which we are denied. Quarrels and humiliations; sensations of self-confidence, jealousy and desire; even pulse rates, alcohol levels, menstrual cycles – like judge and jury, the psychologist usually gains access to such events only at second, third or fourth hand.

Consider, again, Dyson and his performance on television. This was ambiguous, in the sense that as many meanings were attached to it as there were spectators watching him; and ambiguous, too, in that these meanings changed, coalesced and changed again over time. As we saw, Dyson's own perception of the matter changed dramatically in the middle of the night, and gradually reversed itself as a consensus about his performance took shape. The other spectators each had their own distinctive perception: Jannie, Bob, Lord Boddy, Samantha Lightbody from the B.B.C. The consensus that his performance was a success was itself fragile, and one about which a number of people, Dyson included, had surreptitious reservations. It collapsed when Dyson was superseded in expert-hood by Erskine Morris. Frayn establishes for us that Erskine is in fact more expert than Dyson:

> They gazed at the screen. Morris appeared on it again, talking about certain social developments he had noticed in the Western Region of Nigeria when he had been out there earlier in the year. His voice flowed on like the smoke rising from his cigarette, steady and unemphatic, but definitely hypnotic.
> 'There goes my future,' said Dyson sadly.

Jannie rubbed his hand.

'Bob's future, too,' he said. 'We're both washouts, Jan.'

Morris cut Lord Boddy off in mid-reminiscence with a deftly-placed Sure sure, and put the chairman right on a couple of points of fact.

'He's good,' whispered Bob.

'He's a nasty little prick,' said Dyson.[3]

Here again though, Frayn is exercising the novelist's God-like powers. In real life, a lasting, incontrovertible consensus about which of two experts is the more expert is not easily achieved.

So much for the public actions of one man, Dyson. But what of the less public acts of two people? Dyson for example being nagged, or thinking he is being nagged, by his wife, Jannie:

'Look, Jannie,' he said reasonably, following her back to the kitchen, 'just *tell* me what it is you're going on about. That's all I ask.'

'I'm not going on about anything, John,' said Jannie.

'Yes, you are, Jannie.'

'No, I'm not, John.'

'Look, we both know we're having an argument! Let's not have another argument about whether we're having an argument or not!'

Jannie gazed into the food cupboard, picking up cereal packets and shaking them to see if they needed replacing.

'There's some coffee in the pot, if you'd like to light the gas,' she said.

Dyson lit the gas absently. It was self-defeating, this sort of nagging, he thought. That's what I really object to. If I haven't the slightest idea what the hell I'm being nagged about, how the hell can I possibly do anything about it?

'Put some milk on, too, will you, John?'

He put some milk on, sighing. I mean, he thought, I know what she's *up* to, all right. I'm not a complete fool. This was the classic method of brainwashing, after all, used by interrogators, priests, and psycho-analysts alike. 'I think you have something you want to tell me' – that's what their technique was. Then they simply waited for you to accuse yourself.

Jannie sat down at one corner of the great kitchen table and began to write a shopping list. Dyson stood by the stove, gazing down at her with serious ferocity.

'Jannie ...' he began.

'Yes, John?'

Dyson stopped, frowning harder.

'Why do you call me John in that tone of voice?' he demanded.

'Don't you like me calling you John?' asked Jannie, not looking up from her shopping list.

'You don't normally go round calling me John all the time.'

She didn't answer. Good God, he thought, I should like to do something that would really make her jump out of her skin for once. He pictured himself smashing both fists down in the middle of the kitchen table, or taking a china jug off the shelf and hurling it across the room. It was absurd that Norman Ward Westerman and Lord Boddy should listen with real deference to his views on Halifax, while at home he couldn't even get a hearing from his own wife. Scribble, scribble, scribble, she went. Eggs, butter, tea, coffee – oh God, the *smallness* of things![4]

In the normal round of duty, the psychologist will never witness an exchange so innocently revealing. His access is through the recollections of the two participants, who, needless to say, will view it in different lights: Dyson as subtle persecution, Jannie as John in one of his 'states'. He must also assess the artificiality his own inquiry creates. Both Dyson and Jannie will present accounts mediated by their perception of him, and their relation to him: specifically, by the extent to which he has their trust. Yet, a problem familiar from psycho-analysis, the greater the trust, the more likely are recollections to be transformed by this new relationship. 'Rapport' is thus two-edged: poor rapport distorts the flow of information, good rapport distorts it too.

What, in any case, is the observer to make of the messages he receives? What is a row? To one couple, a few words spoken by one of the partners in a special tone of voice, followed by silence and tension. To another, shouting that can be heard three doors away, breaking crockery, excoriating abuse. The difficulty lacks a simple solution. And even if husband, wife and psychologist were all to agree that certain events occurred, and that they constituted a row, all that we would know for certain is that three people have brought to bear on this transaction compatible assumptions about what constitutes a row.

Theoretically, this point is critical. Problems of meaning abound whenever one person attempts to understand another he does not know intimately. And when he does know him intimately, they still abound. For their relationship will have generated a context of social rituals, jokes, tacit assumptions, that enable them to negotiate the dangerous patches their relationship contains. Consequently, any agreement they reach may reflect no more than the existence of a common mini-culture between them. Problems of meaning thus affect not just Anglo-Saxon communicating with Zuni, middle class communicating with working class. They arise whenever two people attempt to communicate about aspects of their lives which are other than banal. The intriguing aspect of this semantic quandary is not that it exists in the human sciences but that psychologist, sociologist and anthropologist have conspired so successfully to ignore it.

The extreme case is that of the anthropologist. Member of an economically sophisticated society, he goes off into bush or jungle to appraise a way of life dissimilar to his own in almost every particular. At best, he has a foreigner's grasp of the language, and is usually forced to communicate through interpreters or middlemen: people marginal to both the cultures in question. The fruits of this curious interaction are then published as objective evidence about the primitive culture observed. Discussed with exemplary candour by at least one of the subject's founding fathers, W. H. R. Rivers, such lacunae have since been glossed over by anthropologists preoccupied, like their neighbours the psychologists, with their own emergent professionalism.*

Ideally, like the anthropologist, the psychologist and sociologist also try to grasp the lives other people lead, not merely intuitively (as the novelist can) but by reference to some explicit model or theory or set of distinctions. Our semantic difficulties are less obvious; and we also have the advantage – if such it is – of greater freedom in whom we approach and in how we approach them. But our freedom seems in the event to have daunted us: we have shrunk back under the protection of our expertise. To a degree that is astounding, academic psychologists have shunned not only contact with people, but ideas about people that they would naturally derive from such contacts. We dwell in a world of simple abstractions. Anthropology seems at times to have degenerated into an algebra of

---

* As a result, observer-effects in anthropology are treated at the level of gossip. The stock example among my Cambridge students was Margaret Mead's finding about the Arapesh: that both men and women among them tended to conform to the pattern of the American woman. Fortune, visiting the Arapesh a few years later, failed to confirm this. My students found it telling that the two investigators had been man and wife, but at the time of Fortune's attempted replication were so no longer.

kinship diagrams; sociology into an unending disquisition on the notion of social class. But in psychology, the flight from our 'historically constituted subject-matter' is altogether more extreme. And the tendency, once again, is exemplified by the mental testers.

The statistical theories of intelligence, impressive accomplishments in their way, were constructed by men who in many cases eschewed all but the most marginal contacts with the creatures their theories were about. Even the standard testing session, the root of the whole enterprise, has only too often been left to others: research assistants, teachers, students, volunteers – any technically competent person who will take the brunt of direct personal contact. Granted such shyness, we might picture experts on intelligence poring in libraries over the more subtle manifestations of human thought – avid readers who are connoisseurs of the arts, and well-versed in science, distilling for us special insights into the mind's mysterious ways. But even this is not so. Mental testers, for the last fifty years at least, have shown no more interest in such matters than have, say, biochemists or mechanical engineers. Indeed, having the key to such mysteries in their statistical models, they have shown if anything less interest. And the literature they have created is as a consequence a monument to all that is hermetic and inward-looking.

The rest of us have followed this pattern in greater or lesser degree. We conduct our experiments on captive audiences: classes of schoolchildren, or of our own students. Or we distribute questionnaires by post. Or we lift people from the context in which they live, and set them down in our departments and laboratories – where we are at ease, and they are not. Or we avoid the human race altogether, and settle for the monkey or the rat. In self-defence, of course, we point to the profound technical difficulties of a more natural approach, and to the risk that fragile theory can easily be swamped by the wealth of human individuality. Both arguments carry weight. But it is symptomatic of the condition into which we have lapsed that our shelves should sag with works that warn us against any loss of 'objectivity', but scarcely a pamphlet to indicate the far greater, more insidious danger of encapsulation.

By now, the damage is done. Both intellectually and psychically, we have retreated; and, as Sigmund Koch shrewdly remarked, we have formed 'rationales for so doing which could only invite further retreat'. It is as though contact with raw, smelly people were irrelevant to the patterns in our heads; as though they might damage or contaminate us. Yet even within the enclave we have constructed for ourselves, we still cannot shake off the bogey of semantics. The moment we set out to explore the relation of general concepts to the real world, we are beset. A practical example makes this plain. We can profess an interest, as I have done, in the general notion of authority; and ask students to relate certain authority figures – father, policeman, judge, army officer, schoolmaster – to certain pairs of adjectives – hard/soft, warm/cold, valuable/ worthless, and so on. Seemingly straightforward, the task is fraught with hidden complication. If, to take a simple instance, American students see policemen as harder, colder and less valuable than do their British contemporaries, this may be because their systems of value differ; or because American and British policemen differ; or, the most likely explanation, because both values and policemen differ together.

But to imply that American and British policemen differ 'objectively', as well as in their 'image', is itself a more nebulous proposition than it seems. The American carries a gun, the British does not. The American is the more likely to take bribes and to kill civilians. But the causal connections between image and behaviour may prove complex. Both may stem from more general assumptions about figures in authority that members of the two societies make. Americans, students and policemen alike, may assume that all agents of authority are, of their very nature, harsh and corruptible; whereas the British may expect greater honesty and restraint. And both sets of assumption may stem, in their turn, from the political traditions of the countries in question; one based on the ideals of free enterprise and individual endeavour, the other more hierarchic.* Policemen may seem to differ 'objectively' yet occupy semantic niches that are analogous. On the other hand, the very definition of those niches, the words Americans and British use in discussing questions of authority, are themselves loose from any firm foundation. There is no semantic constant to which we can appeal. Add to this the likelihood that American and British students will respond differently to questions about the police, and the methodological brew is dense, to say the least. And the difficulties that apply to Americans and British, students and policemen, apply in principle to any two people whose experience of life has been in any significant way dissimilar: that is to say, any two people at all.

Yet as long as he remains seriously concerned to understand the world about him, as long as he avoids the temptation to play the social roles of 'scientist' or 'wise man', it is this methodological brew that the psychologist must stir. His attempt is to reconstruct the lives of other people in his work; and this remains so whether he is the harshest of empiricists or the most glutinous of the humane. There is no easy way out. And the efforts of reconstruction he makes are similar, in most of their essential respects, whatever the stance from which he begins. Whether he acknowledges it or not, even the least intuitive of psychologists shares the constraints not only of his softer neighbours, but also those of the novelist or even of the

---

* 'The permanent attributes of "policing" are the arbitrary, the unpredictable, and the unjust.' Thus the American, Morse Peckham, in *Art and Pornography*.[5] I would be surprised if many inhabitants of the British Isles perceived the mechanisms of social control in quite these terms.

painter. The sociologist Robert Nisbet has pointed to three such:

> ... first, awareness of the element of *art* that lies in all efforts to grasp reality, no matter how undergirded by pretentious methodologies and computer systems these efforts may be; second, that, however one proceeds, with whatever degree of objectivity and devotion to truth, he cannot escape the limitations imposed by the *form* of his enquiry; and third that many of the words through which social scientists, humanists, and others approach reality are unalterably metaphoric.[6]

On the face of it, such embarrassments may all seem grist to the behaviourist's mill: the fancier forms of the art damned by their own admission. Stick, he may urge, to the hard facts: age, sex, social class, educational achievement, marriage and divorce rates, fertility, the incidence of disease and crime, rental values, and what have you. The argument is beguiling; and I succumb to it several times a year. But it remains chimerical. There is a profound pleasure to be had in hitching interpretations to data such as these. They form our anchor in times of need. But, in isolation, they are meaningless; and we tend, in any case, to absorb ourselves in playing statistical tunes upon them. Worse, if we are not scrupulous, we find ourselves edging round to the view that such simple facts are in some important sense basic; that people are reducible to the forms of evidence about them that we find it easiest to collect. The first, statistical, tendency is a form of scholasticism to which we are all subject in greater or lesser degree. The second, reductive, one is ideology, crude and brazen.

A New Root Metaphor 11

'A corner of nature seen through a temperament'; the definition suits my view of psychology quite well. It also suits my
view that the definer should have been a nineteenth-century
novelist, Emile Zola; and that I should have come across it
in Gombrich's outstanding work on the visual arts, *Art and
Illusion*.[1] What the definition lacks, for painting and literature
as for psychology, and what Gombrich amply supplies, is the
sense of a discipline as a cultural entity, with its own language,
symbols, conventions. My argument has been that as a cultural
entity, psychology has had the misfortune to cut itself off both
from its neighbours, and also, to an alarming extent, from the
raw material out of which its own fabric should properly be
built. Psychology should stretch continuously – as until quite
recently it did stretch – from the creative and scholarly arts on
the one hand, to the established sciences on the other; and it
should overlap generously with both.

If we are to recover our pristine vigour, a major change is in
store; not at the periphery, nor in detail, but at our corporate
nub – a change in our conception of what we are about. And
such a change must hinge on the emergence of a new model
with which we can epitomize ourselves; a new root metaphor
from which our more day-to-day activities will flow.

Before indulging in a positive proposal about what shape
our new root metaphor should take, I would like briefly to talk
about bodies of knowledge as a whole. For the belief that
bodies of knowledge are lawful, cultural entities, and that they
develop their own structure and momentum, is one that both

philosophers of science and sociologists of knowledge now accept as commonplace. As far as the physical and biological sciences are concerned, their case is unanswerable. As both Kuhn and Merton have pointed out, multiple discovery is normal in an established field. An insight occurs there not to the occasional genius, but to dozens of individuals almost simultaneously, although they may be working in mutual isolation. Ideas that a few years previously were inaccessible present themselves, more or less at the same historical moment, to all those scientists who ride the crest of a particular research wave. What is unthinkable in one decade is grasped in the next by the most athletic, and consigned in the one that follows to the status of platitude.

I doubt, though, whether this analysis can be applied to the behavioural and social sciences. Although the psychology I learnt at Oxford has already acquired a period charm, and the research I watched in Cambridge is already slipping into the history of its subject, the impression is one of impermanence. There is change, certainly; one vogue follows another. But the movement is less cumulative than cyclic; and more subject than in other sciences to that 'Great Prime Mover of all intellectual activity, the *Zeitgeist*, without whom no man would think as he does, nor have his thoughts make sense'.[2]

In an excellent article, Jerome Kagan, the Harvard psychologist, offers spontaneous evidence of growth from within; of a radical, non-reversible shift in the way that psychology is conceived:

> The psychology of the first half of this century was absolutistic, outerdirected and intolerant of ambiguity. When a college student carries this unholy trio of traits he is called authoritarian, and such has been the temperament of the behavioral sciences. But the era of authoritarian psychology may be nearing its dotage, and the decades

ahead may nurture a discipline that is relativistic, oriented to internal processes, and accepting of the idea that behavior is necessarily ambiguous.

Less than seventy-five years ago biology began to drift from the constraints of an absolute view of events and processes when she acknowledged that the fate of a small slice of ectodermal tissue depended on whether it was placed near the area of the eye or the toe. Acceptance of the simple notion that whether an object moves or not depends on where you are standing is a little over half a century old in a science that has five centuries of formalization. With physics as the referent in time, one might expect a relativistic attitude to influence psychology by the latter part of the twenty-third century. But philosophical upheavals in one science catalyse change in other disciplines and one can see signs of budding relativism in the intellectual foundations of the social sciences.[3]

By 'relativistic', Kagan means that both the internal state of the individual and his context must be part of any defining statement about him. This is surely right. But, in my view, Kagan has made the causes of this shift seem too rational, and he has drawn back from its full implication. The causes of the conceptual shift must lie, I would have thought, not primarily within psychology, nor in the catalytic influence of neighbouring disciplines, but in the more general cultural shift in our attitudes to authoritative knowledge. And in this new mood of hostility to dogma, the legitimacy of the psychologist's own position is itself for the first time suspect: he is no longer assumed to be above his own laws. If the principle of relativism is to apply at all, it must encompass not only the people psychologists study, but the psychologists who do the studying.

This is a state of affairs defined in the first law of meta-psychology: Hudson's Law of Selective Attention to Data – first devised half seriously, but here presented in all earnestness, or almost so. The Law's first proposition takes the vague but potent notion of relevance, and uses it to assert what the subject-matter of psychology ought to be. Namely:

I. That psychology is relevant inasmuch as it illuminates men's ideologies. It is relevant, in other words, to the extent that it examines the nature and tests the validity of the assumptions we use in making sense of the world about us.

Relevance, in other words, is accepted as desirable; and is given a reasonably specific meaning. The need is for research on men's assumptions about human nature; on the schemata we use, intuitively, in interpreting what both we and our neighbours do. In more down-to-earth terms, the Law calls for research that is useful, not in the servile sense of providing information on which policy-makers can make policy, but in that it explores the strengths and weaknesses of the assumptions that policy-makers make.

Next, the Law points to a dilemma. It asserts:

II. That the greater the ideological relevance of research, the greater the likelihood that the research worker doing it will pay selective attention to the evidence he collects.

Such selectivity will be systematic, needless to say, reflecting the psychologist's own commitment – buried or blatant – to the issues in question. And the dilemma leads us to a choice: between research that is dispassionate but irrelevant on the one hand, and, on the other, research that is relevant but untrustworthy.

Next, the Law indicates two of the tell-tale signs of ideological commitment in research:

III. That the greater the research worker's ideological
involvement in his task, the more he will tend to adopt an
extreme posture, as very hard or very soft; and the more
strenuously will he appeal to external authority – if hard,
to the authority of Science; if soft, to humane virtues like
Democracy and Individuality.

Next, the Law establishes psychology in its political and
social context. It asserts:

IV. That ideological commitment in research increases at
times of political stress in society at large. And research not
merely reflects that stress; it contributes to it.

The point here is not that the psychologist is necessarily power-
less in the grip of cultural and political processes; rather that he
is an integral part of them. It is precisely with his power to
control his exchange with the wider society that the next, and
originally the final, assertion of the Law deals. It proposes:

V. That a psychology which is both relevant and dispassionate becomes possible only when the psychologist
and his preoccupations are included as part of what psychologists seek to explain.

The rest of this chapter is an attempt to make the implications
of this last proposition clear. For while systematic truth about
human nature remains the psychologist's goal, the Law signals
a major departure from traditional, absolutist conceptions of
the psychologist's work. It takes Kagan's view of a relativistic
psychology, and includes the psychologist himself as an element
in it. And although this may seem at first sight a parochial

L

issue, a problem for psychologists, the Law in fact embraces all systematic attempts to understand human nature, and each of the various academic traditions from which we may choose to begin.

Superficially, Hudson's Law might seem to suggest a state of anarchy, in which all prejudices carried equal weight, and only trivial research could hope to be value-free. But in fact, in pointing to the inadequacies of the old conception of psychology, it tacitly outlines a new one – a model in which the investigator is denied any special authority or status, and in which (as in life) the elements interact and interdepend. In the past, scientific psychologists have relied on a model or metaphor of their own activities that is naively objective, in the sense that it admits only those elements that the sternest empiricist would admit: observable behaviour, a measurement technology, data, and theories that have been logically defined. If I am right, this 'behaviour + measurement technology + data + logical theory' model has the status of a fiction; a fiction that can no longer be justified in terms of its usefulness of the fruits it is about to bear. The hundreds of millions of research man-hours that it has inspired have yielded astonishingly little in the way of enduring insights or socially valuable skills. The traditional conception is more an aesthetic, a vision of a technological paradise that society might eventually become – and in which the psychologist would enjoy special power. In its place, I would like to propose a root metaphor for the psychologist at work that is of such unpretentiousness as scarcely to qualify as a metaphor at all. Hudson's Law thus bears an appendix, a codicil:

VI. That the psychologist should envisage his work as a process wherein *one person becomes acquainted with others.*

Obviously, this notion of human acquaintanceship cannot define psychology exhaustively. Rather, it indicates its gist;

where its centre of gravity should lie. And like any other epitomizing utterance – any schema that seeks to describe what could exist, but does not exist now – this one has both its strengths and its limitations.

First, in rapid succession, its good points. It enables us to focus on the life-span, the *biography*, of the individual as the site of psychological explanation. It removes from the psychologist his God-like exemption from subjectivity of judgment. It accepts the practical constraints of working with other people, rather than implying that these should be mysteriously wafted away. It places centrally what belongs centrally – the act of making sense; and it does so without diminishing the significance of behaviour, either as evidence, or as part of what this act of making sense seeks to encompass or explain.

For, at this early stage especially, the weight of the metaphor is not primarily interpersonal, but *interpretative*. Interpretations are its basic concern: interpretations, the interpretation of interpretations (both our own and other people's), and – especially in teaching – their transmission and control. In a word, the metaphor is *hermeneutic*.* And we, all of us, are interpreters, '*hermeneuts*' – creatures who pan for sense in the muddy waters of human transaction, and who, if we are interested in people, collect this sense into the bundles of remembered event, belief and fantasy that constitute the human biography.

Where, schematically speaking, psychology has in the past been conceived as contact between two sets of objects – or logical systems – via a measurement technology, it would in future be seen as mutual infiltration between at least two systems of meaning: one in the mind of the plain-man-to-be-explained, the other in the mind of the person-dressed-as-a-psychologist. One set of meanings, one set of interpretations, are those the plain man evolves in making sense of his own

---

* 'Hermeneutics': the art or science of interpretation, esp. of Scripture. *Oxford English Dictionary*. The term is used by the new theologians, but this should not daunt us.[4]

experience and surroundings – including psychology and psychologists. The other is the set the psychologist evolves to make sense of plain men and his own relation to them. Such infiltration, needless to say, is mediated by the observable behaviour of the two participants – what they say and do. But the interpretations they reach are not reducible to such actions, nor are such actions interesting until interpretation is given to them.*

Where, in the past, scientific psychologists have tried to convince us that our thoughts are ephemeral and in some important sense 'unreal', the metaphor of acquaintanceship reasserts the propriety of thought about thought. It echoes Michael Polanyi's assertion that 'since I regard the significance of a thing as more important than its tangibility, I shall say that minds and problems are more real than cobblestones'.[5] Where psychologists have deemed themselves categorically different from plain men, being possessed of a higher magic known as the Scientific Method, the metaphor dwells on the interpretative lot both plain men and psychologists share. The psychologist's musings may eventually take on a formal shape – in flow charts and formulae – and may be checked systematically against the evidence; conversely, certain plain men may achieve an intuitive depth of insight that professional psychologists lack. But both are hermeneuts, and their efforts to achieve understanding are essentially of the same sort.

What sets the psychologist off from the plain man is his self-consciousness about his methods; and this should scarcely surprise us, because his difficulties here are very great. Occasionally, he can act as a fly on the wall; sometimes, especially to begin with, he can use documentary sources. But normally, if he is to collect evidence about people, he is forced to create a

---

* If it could have one, the metaphor's patron philosopher might well turn out to be Merleau-Ponty. Or, rather, some transfiguration of Merleau-Ponty who shared his interests but wrote less turgid prose.

special, supernumerary relationship with them. The difficulty then arises that the aspects of themselves that plain men and women display in this special context may differ from any they have displayed before. Nor can we assume that the two systems of meaning – the psychologist's and the plain man's – will automatically mesh. Each person's view is rooted in his own biography; and the greater the difference between any two biographies, the more an effort at mutual understanding takes on a cross-cultural character. Here, the personal needs and commitments of the psychologist become crucial. He may misinterpret what he observes; and, advertently or inadvertently, specifically or more diffusely, he may alter it.

Typically, human beliefs (the metaphor of acquaintanceship, not least) are beliefs about what other people do or should believe. Concern with interpretation leads inexorably, in other words, to concern with the control of interpretation. The processes whereby we control the contents of other people's minds are thus not simply part of the psychologist's subject-matter; inasmuch as he publishes or teaches, they are his stock-in-trade. So if anthropology can be said to deal with the description of belief systems, and sociology with the description of their control, the metaphor of acquaintanceship implies a seamless fabric of inquiry in which anthropology, sociology and psychology – the sciences of society and of the individual – are indissolubly linked.

Like any other metaphor, that of human acquaintanceship is open, of course, to misinterpretation, and especially to interpretation that is too literal. It would be quite wrong to infer from it, for example, that all psychological information should in future be collected face to face, eyeball to eyeball. Or, equally, that there is no longer any call to collect evidence in a clean and orderly way – there is a call, in fact, for far greater care, not less. It would be quite wrong, too, to infer that no purely behavioural work on human beings is worth doing; or, if it is worth doing, that it should not count as psychology. On the other hand, the metaphor does imply that behavioural evidence – about hormonal secretions, or patterns of cortical activity, or patterns of social activity – is most likely to be of value, and to count for academic purposes as psychology, if it is related to aspects of the individual's life that are meaningful to him: his work, marriage, ambitions, anxieties, and so on.

A further drawback of the metaphor is that it might lead to a degree of self-consciousness about the social psychology of psychology that was inbred. However the real danger is that this new conception will be judged, despite urgent disavowals, in terms of just those primitive systems of meaning that it seeks to transcend. That it will be seen as a movement away from the hard towards the soft; an attempt to assert woolly humanitarian values at the expense of clear-headed and rational ones. Such a fate would be more than usually galling, the rationale of this new view being precisely its appeal to methodological rigour. What is denied is either the intellectual vitality or the practical usefulness of scientism; of a fictitious posturing that exaggerates the psychologist's present competence, and obscures both the slackness of his logic, and the pernicious side-effects of his labour.

The adoption of any such new conception of psychology will be met, as Thomas Kuhn would predict, with fierce resistance from within the profession.* It will also lead to substantial redistributions of effort. Activities now seen as significant will appear trivial, and vice versa. As a discipline, psychology will take as its core activities now treated as off-shoots: social, educational, developmental, semantic and trans-actional research. Traditional concerns, such as learning theory

* It is not clear to me whether the metaphor of acquaintanceship qualifies as a 'paradigm' in Kuhn's sense or not.[6] Nor do I see whether a 'paradigm change' in the human sciences turns, as it is claimed to in the physical sciences, on concrete examples of new work; or, as in politics, philosophy and religion, on charismatic personalities and revolutionary texts. My hunch is that we shall need all three.

based on rats and monkeys, and the more primitive aspects of human perception, will find their natural homes in departments of physiology, zoology, and animal behaviour – and, with luck, the more mindless among the statistical analyses in which we are now in danger of drowning will find no natural home at all. Recruitment to the profession will begin to favour those whose technical abilities are matched by perceptiveness in personal matters. And the teaching of psychology will itself become the focus of searching inquiry. Whilst links will be retained with those biological and physical sciences that are actively concerned with the prediction of human action – genetics, for example, animal behaviour, endocrinology, computer simulation – the identification of psychology in fantasy with the nineteenth-century conception of physics would evaporate. Psychology would belong again, as it did a hundred years ago, indeed as it did only fifty years ago in this country, with all those other academic specialities whose subject-matter is Man.

Like every other aspiring innovation, the metaphor of acquaintanceship and the notion of the psychologist as a hermeneut demand a pedigree; and, in broad outline, this is easily traced. There is, first of all, the emphasis he places on the human biography. This wholesome concern for what people actually do with their lives – as scientists, politicians, salesmen, husbands, parents, students – rather than simply with their answers to psychological tests, is something that has been lost almost entirely from psychology. Evidence about people's lives is now treated as though it were vaguely unseemly. Yet this directness was central to Galton's work, and remains the most impressive feature of it. The *Zeitgeist* permitting, one longs for its return.

Secondly, there is the interest the hermeneutic conception of psychology implies in the schematizing tendency of human thought. This is now manifest in linguistics and anthropology –

one thinks for example of Chomsky and Lévi-Strauss; it was dominant in *Gestalt* psychology, and in the work of Bartlett; and goes back eventually to the Continental philosophy of Hegel, Kant and Descartes. There is an important respect in which the present view lies outside the Continental structural tradition, even so; namely its concern with content rather than merely with form. It focuses on what, in our eyes and theirs, people's lives mean.*

The assumption of the transactional nature of our knowledge about other people has an obvious source in Laing, Goffman, and phenomenology; and also, in the United States, in the work of Carl Rogers. But it has another source, too, in Rosenthal's research on observer-effects in the behavioural sciences: he shows that the psychologist's expectations influence not only the interpretation of his data, but the data themselves, even when rats rather than people are his victims. And the respectful appreciation that the metaphor reflects for the cultural determinants of perceived meaning has Rivers as distant precursor – his studies, for example, of cross-cultural differences in visual illusions; but more recently, and more powerfully, McClelland's work on motive acquisition, and Kuhn's thinking about the internal structure of scientific knowledge.

Perhaps the metaphor's most central characteristic is the attitude to scientific authority that it expresses – the belief that this must be earned, not pre-empted. The idea of a unilateral exemption for psychologists from psychological and social laws is rejected; but so, too, implicitly, is a relativistic free-for-all.

---

* There are affinities here with the semantic psychology of Osgood and Kelly; and following Kelly in this country, Bannister and Mair. Also the 'ethnomethodology' of Garfinkel, and the sociology of Goffman. Mair has recently proposed a 'conversational' model for psychology, which in many respects resembles the metaphor of acquaintanceship, though it suffers a little, I feel, from being advanced in too literal a form.[7] What is lacking in each of these approaches, to my eye at least, despite the excellence of their emphasis on life as it is construed, is any interest in the systematic collection of evidence about what people actually do. They are too remote from the evidence that a good biographer or social historian or gossip finds it natural to collect.

And although this attitude undoubtedly has a long and reputable history, I can trace it no farther than to contact with my own students. Firstly, to their egalitarianism, and their knowledge of systematic sociology. And secondly, set against this, to my own disbelief that all human efforts are ultimately of equal worth; my faith that somewhere, over the rainbow, there lies a state of grace in which a truth can be reached that is not itself a purely political event.

There remains, once all this is said, the question of values. This is more complicated, for one of the most irritatingly persistent of the legacies that Ayer brought to England from Vienna in the 1930s is the assumption that all forms of inquiry are either an expression of prejudice, or scientific, and hence value-free. This tenet has recently been attacked by the radical left: those who claim that all human activity is of its very nature either value-laden or trivial. And the debate is unenlightening because it is drawn, as so often, around a distinction that is itself falsely posed. For issues of value enter research in a variety of ways – logically distinct, but at present blithely confused.

Research, first of all, has its roots – academic, financial, political, social. Different combinations of these make different problems seem worth resolving – the case of race and I.Q. is a good illustration of this, seeming vital to some, trivial to others. And granted the phenomena of human learning, we must all be loyal to (and bounded by) our intellectual origins to greater or lesser degree: as a psychologist, let us say, against the sociologists over the road; as a plain man of good sense, against the woolly or the jargon-ridden; or as a scholar up his ivory tower defending the decencies against the agencies of social change.

Next, and overlapping, there are the questions about the assumptions implicit in research: the personal and social qualities it surreptitiously endorses – the convergent personality, workers' control, or the 'integrated day'; and the standards of legitimacy to which it subscribes – the assumption, for example, that psychological research must contain statistics, or that social research is trivial unless it is based on systematic theory.*

Lastly, there are the questions about the effects of research: its academic consequences as far as the professional advancement of the investigator, his department or his subject are concerned; its contribution to the unfathomable pool of public misinformation; its social and political impact – heightening racial tension, say, or reducing the number of university places; the human characteristics it promotes – an increase, let us say, in parental permissiveness, and subsequent anomie among the young; and, perhaps most important of all, its influence on our assumptions about the limits of legitimate inquiry, the very existence of certain sorts of research making it easier to ask some questions and more difficult to ask others.

It is a little hard to conceive of research that would be value-free in all these respects; or of a research worker who would wish his work to be so. The question then becomes one of detail. And in the case of the metaphor of acquaintanceship, it is clear that at different levels of analysis, different, and at times conflicting, values are invoked. In terms of its academic roots, and of the general character of the research it would promote, the metaphor embodies – to use Norman Brown's shorthand – both erotic and aggressive modes: erotic in its concern for the exploration of the world of the other; aggressive in its presupposition that some semblance of order can eventually be reached. At the level of method, it serves the same values that inform all academic inquiry: dispassion, rigour. And these would seem, in Nietzsche's terms, to be eminently Apollonian concepts, which fall within the sphere of Thanatos. Yet the

* Questions of value merge here with questions of style: whether, for example, one is an 'explorer', following a fertile line; or an 'administrator', laying down a legislative grid. Whether one's life is spent looking for the Nile's source, or in bringing order to the territories of the Queen.

endeavour as a whole must be judged. The notion of human science that exists as an end in itself, irresponsible, will no longer do. The terms of reference here can only, I think, be erotic, humane: the extent to which the research enriches or impoverishes the experiential life of human beings. And in order that judgments of this sort may be made, psychology must produce both the evidence and the criteria for its own evaluation. For without the academic pursuit of psychology, the notions of the enrichment or impoverishment of human life can be assessed only in the light of our individual prejudices.

In crucial respects, in other words, the metaphor affirms conflicting values: passion and dispassion. The question then arises of how they fit together. The Oxford philosopher's solution is to make dispassion king. Norman Brown, on the other hand, castigates Freud for following a similar path; for asserting the reality principle and maturity as the highest virtues. He also rejects the possibility that the erotic and the aggressive, the passionate and the dispassionate, can enter into a dialectical, Hegelian relation. And like Marcuse, he ends by plumping for one of the argument's wings at the expense of the other; for an erotic rather than an aggressive construction of reality.

Yet this last move seems short-sighted, even confused; as if an empiricist's fear of paradox, though alien, had enveloped both writers in the end. For even if we leave the problems of the psychologist and social scientist aside, and concentrate on what more ordinary people do, the war between Eros and Thanatos is not one that either can or should be resolved. They are impulses, values, that act on one another in ways that suggest total interdependence. Even at the humblest, most physical level, at that of sexuality rather than sensibility, the mutual action of Eros and Thanatos is clear to see. Sexual intercourse per se, as practised among dogs, or baboons, or gorillas, leaves no cultural residue; no books, no poems, no paintings; no Freud, and come to that, no Kinsey either. Yet without such a residue, we should live in a world of blind impulse, transient sensation: a world of grunts and spasms. Without the fruits of sublimation, the instinctual life is without meaning. Intuitively, we know when we glimpse them that certain aspects of the personal life are worth living for. And these touchstones, or reference points, are, as often as not, works of art: cryptographic records of our urge to petrify experience, to render it lifeless in ways that make experience more telling.*

In asking, then, that the intellectual and personal halves of our life, or our science, should be knit together, we are asking for something at once profoundly important and profoundly complex. At one extreme, the actor who can bring the world of others alive for us may be able to mimic every form of sensual refinement, but experience none at first hand. And at the other, desiccated scholars, the Mr Casaubons of this world, may contribute to knowledge in those singular ways that reduce materially the desiccation of others. Freud, let us remember, is said to have lived a life largely devoid of sexual passion. And Rilke, with whom this work began, was inextricably emotionally confused.† Yet from this unpromising soil sprang an utterance – the sonnet – that serves as an exemplar of what this book has been striving circuitously to say; a model of how the contents of the human mind should be conceived by those who meddle in them: the unicorn fed, not with corn, but with the possibility of being; the brow that put forth a horn; the creature that stole whitely up to a maid, to be within the silver mirror and in her.

* For my taste, this 'paradox of petrification' is expressed most vividly in porcelain. Two groups of figures come to mind. One, a pair of lovers, made at the Chelsea factory, and now in the British Museum: a bucolic vision, some distance removed from cow-pats, and a million miles from slaughter-houses and battery hens. The other, made at Sèvres, is technically more assured, and altogether more sly: two teenage Ledas looking, curious but composed, at a distinctly sexual Swan.[8]

†That strange woman, Lou Andreas-Salomé, his mistress and also Nietzsche's, refers in her *Journal* to the 'totally disorganised' nature of his personal life: his 'bisexuality' which impaired his 'full enjoyment of normal sexual intercourse'; and his 'recourse to self-gratification' that aggravated 'his essentially noxious hostility to the body'.[9]

The Experiential Core 12

What is lacking in Rilke is any acknowledgment of the earthy. He often described himself as 'a mirror'; yet, on the evidence of his poetry, he found it difficult to countenance people blankly as they were. Consequently, the beauty he offers us is a little effete, weak without its 'origin in beastly desire'. Also lacking is any hint of the banana skin that awaits us when we hazard the high-flown; of how solemn analysis can collapse, at the blink of an eye, into the kinds of platitude that old school mottoes express.* And again, of how startling new insights can evaporate, becoming, in Stephen Vizinczey's phrase, no more than a change in the form of our immutable ignorance. To find beauty, beastly desire, and banana skins, one is forced back in time, stereotypically to Shakespeare; or forwards, to the art of the present day – the sculptor Claes Oldenburg for example:

> I am for an art that embroils itself with the everyday crap and still comes out on top ... that imitates the human, that is comic, if necessary, or violent ... that takes its form from the lines of life itself, that twists and extends and accumulates and spits and drips, and is heavy and coarse and blunt and sweet and stupid as life itself.[1]

Most fittingly of all, perhaps, one moves to the art of the baroque: an art that dwelt on the reconciliation of opposites.

* One that has stalked me throughout this text: *Vincit qui patitur*, he conquers who suffers.

Superficially, this led to puns and conceits; more profoundly to an art in which conflicting ideas resonate on one another; human and divine love, the physical and the spiritual, the earthly and the sublime. Perhaps the proudest work of this period is a sculptural tableau, Bernini's *St Teresa* in the church of Santa Maria de la Vittoria in Rome. I would like to consider it briefly, partly because this, at a humble level, has been a baroque book. But partly, too, because it carries us back to what must become, I believe, the human scientist's abiding fear: the danger that the very existence of certain sorts of information may reduce the range of experience to which we are open; the danger that, cumulatively, the psychologist's work will serve to fillet Man of his experiential core.

The story of St Teresa of Avila is now a little hackneyed. She was a sixteenth-century Spanish mystic, a founder of religious establishments, and a notable teacher. Her mystical experiences are of special interest for the concreteness with which she describes them:

In his hands I saw a great golden spear, and at the iron tip there appeared to be a point of fire. This he plunged into my heart several times so that it penetrated to my entrails. When he pulled it out, I felt that he took them with it, and left me utterly consumed by the great love of God. The pain was so severe that it made me utter several moans. The sweetness caused by this intense pain is so extreme that one cannot possibly wish it to cease, nor is one's soul then content with anything but God. This is not a physical, but a spiritual pain, though the body has some share in it – even a considerable share. So gentle is this wooing which takes place between God and the soul that if anyone thinks I am lying, I pray God in His goodness, to grant him some experience of it.[2]

It was acknowledged in Bernini's time, as it is still acknowledged today, that St Teresa's ecstasy was simultaneously both a physical and a spiritual event. It is salutary to reflect, for a moment, what would have been made of St Teresa by twentieth-century exponents of sex research. Their view, one feels, would either be falsely pious -- that she fell within the realms of Religion and Art, not Science; or down-to-earth in the extreme. One can picture Masters and Johnson peering earnestly at the saint much as the sculpted citizens of seventeenth-century Rome peer at her from the edge of Bernini's tableau. They would view her as a prize: for, in their own unlovely terms, none of their sample could 'fantasy to orgasm'. One wonders, though, whether St Teresa's ecstasy could have occurred at all if she had had at her elbow a behavioural scientist, explaining to her that her sensations of the sublime were wholesome, and sprang from the physiological state of her 'target organs'. Her condition is one that has been described in the following words:

Female orgasmic experience can be visually identified as well as recorded by acceptable physiologic techniques ... At orgasm, the grimace and contortion of a woman's face graphically express the increment of myotonic tension throughout her entire body. The muscles of the neck and the long muscles of the arms and legs usually contract into involuntary spasm. During coition in supine position the female's hands and feet voluntarily may be grasping her sexual partner. With absence of clutching interest or opportunity during coition or in solitary response to automanipulative techniques, the extremities may reflect involuntary carpopedal spasm. The striated muscles of the abdomen and the buttocks frequently are contracted voluntarily by women in conscious effort to elevate sexual tensions, particularly in an effort to break through from high plateau to orgasmic attainment. The physiologic onset of orgasm is signaled by contractions of the target organs, starting with the orgasmic platform in the outer third of the vagina. This platform, created involuntarily by localized vasocongestion and myotonia, contracts with recordable rhythmicity as the tension increment is released. The inter-contractile intervals recur at 0·8 second for the first three to six contractions ... The number and intensity of orgasmic-platform contractions are direct measures of subjective severity and objective duration of the particular orgasmic experience.[3]

And so on. Behaviourally speaking, it would be just another orgasm. But neither this, nor any extension of it, could account for the experience St Teresa describes. Bodies may look alike, indeed be alike, yet the contents of minds be totally dissimilar.

It is the phenomenological concomitants of behaviour that are of interest: it is faith in the possibility of religious ecstasy that renders religious ecstasy possible. And our ability to distinguish in logic between the behavioural concomitants of experience, and experience itself, is of little help when the experience is lacking.

Bernini himself was a devout Catholic; a man who combined a sensual nature with strong religious convictions. He went to church, it is said, every day during the last forty years of his life, and twice a week took Communion. For him, the ecstasy of St Teresa was both a technical challenge and an exercise in devotion. Dull Protestant tastes may find her repellent; more adventurous spirits, a little staid. To unaccustomed eyes, his sculpted tableau has an air of theatricality. The angel, with spear poised, simpers with a detachment that borders on vacuity. The rays of the sun, the substantial cloud on which Teresa rests, are somewhat in the style of one's local Odeon. But the figure of Teresa herself is like little else in art. Her fingers and toes are long and deathly, the face waxen. The rumple of her garments is turbulent but also lifeless. She is the embodiment – it is normally conceded – of a woman who is having both a religious experience and an orgasm.

Like Rilke, though more robustly, Bernini deals with sex. And, again like Rilke, he uses it both as a medium and a metaphor for purposes altogether more subtle. For Bernini's sculpture, like Rilke's sonnet, is one of the few works of art to transmit a sense of what it is like to occupy another's mind. Both are triumphs of artifice over the most implacable of barriers: that between one mind and another.

This, then, and a little to my surprise, is the perch on which Rilke's image of the girl and the unicorn has finally settled. I feel the need for a view of knowledge, and a means of expressing that view, which will imply that the contents of the mind matter. A view which affirms, as Shepard, the unicorn's chronicler affirmed, that human nature and the ways of human thought are the only subjects that deeply and permanently concern us. Like the unicorn, we are all denizens of the Monarch Thought's dominions. But newcomers have claimed *Lebensraum*; and although the unicorn's remote and solitary strangeness may be safe enough from scholars of the old and gentlemanly school, it is by no means so from the tramplings of the scientistic, convinced beyond the reach of reason that their own questions are best.

Our view of any such matter is bound, I believe, to be incomplete; and bound as well, to some extent, to be idiosyncratic. No one can be right; or know, at least, that he is so. A sentence of F. H. Bradley's in a letter written towards the end of his life to Bertrand Russell catches this sense of an evolving, rational but ultimately personal vision well:

And yet still I must believe that one never does or can find the whole in all its aspects, and that there never after all

M

will be a philosopher who did not reach his truth, after all, except by some partiality and one-sidedness – and that, far from mattering, this is the right and the only way.[4]

And it is fitting that this should have been written by someone whom we, as students, were taught to regard as an irrelevant Edwardian metaphysician, who died before the enlightenment set in. A man who was made to seem infinitely remote, though he lived and worked in Oxford, and died only thirty years before I was there.

Notes

CHAPTER 1. DOPPELGANGER

1. L. Hudson, *Frames of Mind* (London: Methuen, 1968), p. 85.
2. R. M. Rilke, *Sonnets to Orpheus*, translated by J. B. Leishman (London: Hogarth Press, 1949), p. 95.
3. O. Shepard, *The Lore of the Unicorn* (London: Allen and Unwin, 1930).
4. Ibid., p. 38.
5. Ibid., p. 84.
6. Ibid., p. 47.
7. Ibid., p. 48.
8. Ibid., p. 49.
9. R. M. Rilke, *Malte Laurids Brigge*, quoted by Leishman in *Sonnets to Orpheus*, p. 163.
10. M. Douglas, *Purity and Danger* (Harmondsworth: Penguin, 1970).
11. N. O. Brown, *Life Against Death* (London: Sphere Books, 1968), p. 68.

CHAPTER 2. OXFORD PHILOSOPHY

1. A. J. Ayer, *Language, Truth and Logic* (New York: Dover, 1947), p. 33.
2. Ibid., p. 144.
3. S. Hampshire, *Modern Writers and Other Essays* (London: Chatto & Windus, 1969), p. x.

CHAPTER 3. CAMBRIDGE

1. P. Wilkinson, *John Tresidder Sheppard* (King's College, Cambridge, printed privately, 1969), p. 17.
2. Ibid., p. 34.
3. P. Wilkinson, *Frank Ezra Adcock* (King's College, Cambridge, printed privately, 1969), p. 16.

CHAPTER 4. THE FIRST FOURTEEN YEARS

1. L. Hudson and B. Jacot, 'Marriage and Fertility in Academic Life', *Nature*, 229 (1971), p. 31.

2. M. Austin, 'Dream Recall and the Bias of Intellectual Ability', *Nature*, 231 (1971), p. 59.

3. A. Storr, 'The Meaning of Music', *The Times Literary Supplement*, November 20th, 1970.

4. C. Hoffberg and I. Fast, 'Professional Identity and Impulse Expression in Phantasy', *Journal of Projective Techniques and Personality Assessment*, 30 (1966), p. 488.

5. U. Bronfenbrenner, *The Two Worlds of Childhood* (Russell Sage Foundation, 1970), p. 9.

6. E. Goffman, *Encounters* (Indianapolis: Bobbs-Merrill, 1961), p. 41.

CHAPTER 5. THE RADICAL OBJECTION

1. S. Koch, in T. W. Wann, ed., *Behaviorism and Phenomenology* (University of Chicago, 1964), p. 37.

2. O. L. Zangwill, A. Pryce-Jones, ed., *The New Outline of Modern Knowledge* (London: Gollancz, 1956), p. 168.

3. Brown, *Life Against Death*, p. 209.

4. See, for example, R. W. Friedricks, *A Sociology of Sociology* (New York: Free Press, 1970).

5. B. F. Skinner, *Beyond Freedom and Dignity* (New York: Knopf, 1971).

CHAPTER 6. THE SOFT AND THE HARD

1. S. Marcus, *The Other Victorians* (London: Weidenfeld & Nicolson, 1966), p. 25.

2. Quoted by Marcus in *The Other Victorians*, p. 16.

3. W. Young, *Eros Denied* (London: Weidenfeld & Nicolson, 1964), p. 189.

4. C. Baker, *Ernest Hemingway* (London: Collins, 1969).

CHAPTER 7. THE QUESTION OF INDOCTRINATION

1. F. Galton, *Hereditary Genius* (London: Macmillan, 1892), p. 12.

2. D. Lessing, *The Golden Notebook* (Harmondsworth: Penguin, 1964), p. 113.

3. L. S. Hearnshaw, *A Short History of British Psychology* (London: Methuen, 1964).

4. D. E. Broadbent, 'In Defence of Empirical Psychology', *Bulletin of the British Psychological Society*, 1970, p. 95.

5. M. Douglas, *Purity and Danger*; see also B. Bernstein, 'On the Classification and Framing of Educational Knowledge', in M. Young, ed., *Knowledge and Control* (New York: Collier-Macmillan, in press).

6. R. D. Laing, *The Politics of Experience* (Harmondsworth: Penguin, 1967), p. 59.

7. D. Black, the title poem in *The Educators* (London: Cresset Press, 1969).

8. For references to this literature, see Hudson, *Frames of Mind*.

9. From P. A. Schilpp, ed., *Albert Einstein: Philosopher-Scientist* (La Salle, Ill.: Open Court, 1949); quoted by M. R. Parlett, 'The Syllabus-Bound Student', in L. Hudson, ed., *The Ecology of Human Intelligence* (Harmondsworth: Penguin, 1970), p. 281.

10. A. Bullock, *Hitler, a Study of Tyranny* (Harmondsworth: Penguin, 1962), p. 27.

CHAPTER 8. FALSE SCIENCE

1. H. J. Eysenck, *The Scientific Study of Personality* (London: Routledge & Kegan Paul, 1952), p. 267.

2. For full details, see L. Hudson, *Contrary Imaginations* (London: Methuen, 1966), p. 24.

3. A. R. Jensen, 'How Much Can We Boost I.Q. and Scholastic Achievement?', *Harvard Educational Review*, 39 (1969), p. 32.

4. J. Money, 'Two cytogenetic syndromes', *Journal of Psychiatric Research*, 2 (1964), p. 223. Reprinted in L. Hudson, ed., *The Ecology of Human Intelligence*.

5. Ibid., p. 224.

6. Galton, *Hereditary Genius*, p. 12.

7. Ibid., pp. 21, 328, 346.

8. Hampshire, *Modern Writers and Other Essays*, p. xv.

9. Jensen, op. cit., p. 28.

10. Ibid., p. 16.

11. R. Rosenthal and L. Jacobson, *Pygmalion in the Classroom* (New York: Holt, Rinehart and Winston, 1968).

CHAPTER 9. NO SCIENTIST AN ISLAND

1. G. Thomson, *The Education of an Englishman* (Moray House, 1969).

2. Ibid., p. 77.

3. Ibid., p. 78.

4. Ibid., p. 9.

5. W. B. Pomeroy, in R. and E. Brecher, eds., *An Analysis of the Human Sexual Response* (London: Deutsch, 1966), p. 112.

6. Ibid., p. 113.

CHAPTER 10. MEANINGS AND ACTIONS

1. M. J. Frayn, *Towards the End of the Morning* (London: Collins, 1967), pp. 102–5.
2. Ibid., p. 114.
3. Ibid., p. 253.
4. Ibid., p. 138.
5. M. Peckham, *Art and Pornography* (New York: Basic Books, 1969).
6. R. Nisbet, 'Genealogy, Growth and other Metaphors', *New Literary History*, 1 (1969), p. 3.

CHAPTER 11. A NEW ROOT METAPHOR

1. E. H. Gombrich, *Art and Illusion* (London: Phaidon, 1960).
2. E. G. Boring, *Sensation and Perception in the History of Experimental Psychology* (New York: Appleton Century Crofts, 1949), p. xi.
3. J. Kagan, 'On the Need for Relativism', *American Psychologist*, 22 (1967), p. 131.
4. J. M. Robinson and J. B. Cobb, eds., *The New Hermeneutic* (New York: Harper and Row, 1964).
5. M. Polanyi, *The Tacit Dimension* (London: Routledge & Kegan Paul, 1967), p. 33.
6. T. S. Kuhn, *The Structure of Scientific Revolutions* (Chicago University Press, 1962).
7. J. M. M. Mair, 'Psychologists are Human Too', in D. Bannister, ed., *Perspectives in Personal Construct Theory* (New York: Academic Press, 1970). See also H. Tajfel, 'Experiments in a Vacuum', in J. Israel and H. Tajfel, eds., *The Context of Social Psychology* (New York: Academic Press, in press); and D. Ingleby, 'Ideology and the Human Sciences', *Human Context*, 1970, p. 425.
8. See J. L. Dixon, *English Porcelain of the 18th Century* (London: Faber, 1952), plate 1; and W. B. Honey, *French Porcelain* (London: Faber, 1950), plate 70.
9. L. Andreas-Salomé, *The Freud Journal* (London: Hogarth Press, 1964).

CHAPTER 12. THE EXPERIENTIAL CORE

1. C. Oldenburg, in *Catalogue for the Arts Council of Great Britain Exhibition*, Tate Gallery, 1970, p. 11.
2. H. Hibbard, *Bernini* (Harmondsworth: Penguin, 1965), p. 137.

3. W. H. Masters and V. E. Johnson, *Human Sexual Response* (Boston, Mass.: Little, Brown, 1966), p. 128.

4. Quoted in B. Russell, *The Autobiography of Bertrand Russell, 1872–1914,* (London: Allen & Unwin, 1967), p. 225.

Index

academics: *Who's Who* study, 65–70
acquaintanceship metaphor, 162–72
Acton, William, 88–9
Adcock, F. E., 52–3
adolescence, 66–8
aesthetic experience, 26–7, 172–6
agnosticism, 79
American children, 69n
American Psychologist, 75
analytic philosophy, 40
Andreas-Salomé, Lou, 172n
anthropology, 151
Apostles, debating society, 48–50
Armstrong, David, 45
Art and Illusion (Gombrich), 157
Art and Pornography (Peckham), 154n
arts specialists: perception of, 64, 83, 106;
   Who's Who study, 65–70, 87
astrological symbolism, 24
atheism, 79
atomistic philosophy, 39, 41, 80
Aubusson tapestries, 21
Austin, Mark, 65–7
authoritative knowledge, 128, 159
authority, 105, 122, 128, 153–4
Ayer, A. J., 36, 80, 169

Bannister, D., 168n
Bartlett, F. C., 100, 168
behaviour therapy, 111
behavioural psychology, 73, 77, 88, 145–6
Bernini: *The Ecstasy of St Teresa*, 26, 174–177
Black, David, 106, 109n
Bradley, F. H., 177
brain, differences between male and female, 96–7

Brideshead Revisited (Waugh), 48
British Journal of Sociology, 112
Broadbent, Donald, 104
Bronfenbrenner, U., 69n
Brown, Norman, 27, 75, 90, 170–71
Bulletin of the British Psychological Society, 75
Burt, C. L., 124

Cambridge humanism, 49, 53
Cambridge Psychological Laboratory, 53, 99–101
Cambridge psychology, 99–103
Cambridge University, 45–57
career choice, 62–3
Carnap, R., 81
child fixation, 68–9
child psychology, 54
childhood, 16, 66, 67
Chomsky, Noam, 75–6, 79–80, 101, 104, 129–30, 168
Christ, 22–3
chromosomes, 115–20
classification, 105
communication, 150
Concept of Mind, The (Ryle), 36
Continental structuralism, 78–9
Contrary Imaginations (Hudson), 15, 62, 67, 77–8
convergers: *see* divergers
Craik, Kenneth, 101
creativeness, 109
Creativity and Intelligence (Getzels and Jackson), 62

dajja, 22
Dame à la Licorne, La, 21

185

data processing, 63, 64n
Descartes, René, 76, 80, 101, 168
Deutsch, J. A., 42
developmental research, 166
Dewey, J., 80
discipline, 110
divergers and convergers, 62–3; *Who's Who* study of academics, 65–9; teachers' preference, 108
Divided Self, The (Laing), 78, 95
Douglas, Mary, 26, 105
dreams, 65–7

education, 106–8
educational psychology, 54–5
educational research, 166
effeminacy, 89
'ego-boundaries', 67–8
Einstein, Albert, 109
Eleven-plus examination, 111, 131–5
Emmanuel College, Cambridge, 46–47
emotional expression, 67
empiricism, 77, 80, 99, 103–4
equality, 120, 122
Erikson, Erik, 16
Eros and Civilization (Marcuse), 75n
Exeter College, Oxford, 29–30
existentialism, 76
expectation, 25, 71
experimental psychology, 39–40, 74–5, 77, 100, 102, 104
'expressive' approach to life, 87–8
Eysenck, H. J., 112, 122

facts, 39, 124
family interaction, 146
Farrell, Brian, 33
Fast, I., 68n
fertility among academics, 65, 69
figural after-effect, 42
Forster, E. M., 48, 51
Fortune, R. F., 151n
Frames of Mind (Hudson), 15, 17, 63–4, 71, 79, 85
Frayn, Michael, 139–44, 147–9
freedom, 109

Freud, Sigmund, 27, 28, 75n, 90–91, 129, 171–2
function, 98–9

Galton, Francis, 20, 93, 122
Garfinkel, H., 168n
genetics, 80, 115–20
Getzels, J. W., 62, 108n
Goffman, E., 41, 168n
Gombrich, E. H., 157
Graham, Billy, 80

Hampshire, Stuart, 38, 123
hard and soft, 73, 79, 83–92
Harvard Education Review, 114
Hearnshaw, L. S., 100
Hegel, Friedrich, 28, 168
Heisenberg, W. G., 134
Henry, Jules, 78, 106
hermeneutics, 163–4, 167
Heyer, A. W., 42
Himmelweit, H. T., 112n
History of the Royal Society of London, The (Sprat), 104
Hitler, Adolf, 109
Hobbes, Thomas, 109
Hoffberg, C., 68n
Hudson, Liam: at King's College, 15ff; at Edinburgh, 18; at Oxford, 29ff; at Cambridge, 45ff
Hudson's Law of Selective Attention to Data, 160–64
human acquaintanceship: *see* acquaintanceship
human perception: *see* perception
Hume, David, 76, 80
Humphrey, G., 40

identity, sense of, 79
ideological involvement, 161
industrial psychology, 100
infancy, 66–7; *see also* childhood
information theory, 59, 74
Institute of Experimental Psychology (Oxford), 39–40, 99
'instrumental' approach to life, 87–8
intelligence, 57–8, 62, 152

intelligence and race: *see* race and
  intelligence
intelligence tests, 60–62, 93, 124, 129,
  131–4, 152
Interpersonal Perception (Laing), 78
interpretation, 163
interviews, 111–12

Jackson, P. W., 62, 108n
Jacobson, L., 124n
Jensen, A. R., 114–25
Johnson, V. E., 136–7, 175

Kagan, Jerome, 158–9, 161
Kant, Immanuel, 168
Kelly, G. A., 168n
kibbutzim, 87
King's College, Cambridge, 47–8, 50–53
Kinsey, A. C., 135–6, 171–2
Kneale, William, 33–4
Knots (Laing), 78
Knox, John, 109n
Koch, Sigmund, 73–4, 153
Kogan, N., 108n
Kuhn, Thomas, 158, 166

Laing, Ronald, 76–8, 81, 95, 101, 106,
  109, 129, 146, 168
La Mettrie, J., 80
Language, Truth and Logic (Ayer), 36
learning theory, 167
Leavis, F. R., 47, 49
Leibniz, Gottfried Wilhelm, 80
Leishman, J. B., 18
Lessing, Doris, 98n
Lévi-Strauss, Claude, 17, 71, 97, 138, 168
Life Against Death (Brown), 75, 90
life and death instincts, 90–91
linguistic philosophy, 30–43, 81, 130
Livingstone, David, 20
Locke, John, 76, 80
logical positivism, 36
Longest Journey, The (Forster), 51
Lore of the Unicorn, The (Shepard), 20–26

McClelland, David, 168
MacKinnon, 108n

Mair, J. M. M., 168n
male domination, 87
Marcuse, Herbert, 75n, 78, 91, 103, 129,
  171
marriage among academics, 65–70
Marxism, 50, 75n, 103
masculinity, 90, 105
Masters, W. H., 136–7, 175
masturbation, 136
Mead, Margaret, 151n
Medawar, P. B., 40
media, 60, 62, 130
medical profession, 70–71
Merleau-Ponty, Maurice, 37, 97, 164n
Merton, R. K., 158
metaphysics, 35–6, 80
methodologists, 54
Minnesota Multiphasic Personality Inventory, 58
Money, J., 115–25
motivational research, 111
mottoes, 173
mythology, 12, 19, 26–7, 71

Nature, 59, 62
New College, Oxford, 31
New Scientist, 59
Newsweek, 62
Nietzsche, Friedrich, 27–8, 170
Nisbet, Robert, 155
non-verbal reasoning, 61

objectivity, 41
observer effect on observed, 135–8, 151
Oldenburg, Claes, 173
orgasm, 175–7
orthodoxy, 101
Osgood, C. E., 42, 168n
Oxford philosophy, 29–43, 99

'paradigm change', 166n
Peckham, Morse, 154n
Peirce, C. S., 80
perception, 16–17, 43, 62, 71, 76–7, 83–6,
  88, 95–6, 106, 147, 167
personality, 61
'petrification, paradox of', 172

phenomenology, 76, 80
physiology, 100
Piaget, Jean, 55
poets, psychic lives of, 68n
Polanyi, Michael, 164
polar concepts, 17
polemics, 111
policemen, 153-4
political stress, 161
Politics of Experience, The (Laing), 78
Pomeroy, W. B., 135-6
Powell, Anthony, 53
press and television media, 60, 62, 130
psyche functions, 85
psychoanalysis, 112-13
psychologist, perception of, 85, 127-8
puritanism, 90
purity and virtue, 105
Pygmalion in the Classroom (Rosenthal and Jacobson), 124n

Quarterly Journal of Experimental Psychology, 62
Quinton, Anthony, 36

Rabelais, 20, 26
race and intelligence, 113-14; Jensenism, 114-25, 169
relativistic psychology, 158-61
religious ecstasy, 175-7
Rilke, Rainer Maria: sonnet on girl and the unicorn, 18-28, 57, 68n, 71-2, 172-3, 177
Rivers, W. H. R., 100, 151, 168
Rodin, 26
Rogers, Carl, 168
Rosenthal, R., 123-4
Russell, Bertrand, 37, 80, 177
Russian children, 69n
Ryle, Gilbert, 36

St Teresa of Avila, 174-7
Sanity, Madness and the Family (Laing), 78
Sartre, Jean-Paul, 29, 37, 76, 97, 101
Schlick, M., 81
science: authority of, 105; expression of progress, 92; snobbery of, 53-6, 106

scientists: academic record of, 59; perception of, 64, 83, 90, 106; Who's Who study, 65-70, 87
Scottish education, 109n
selective attention to data, 160
Self and Others, The (Laing), 78
semantic psychology, 166, 168n
sexes, psychological differences between, 97
sexual abstinence, 88
sexuality, 68, 135-6, 171-2, 175
Shepard, Odell, 20-26, 177
Sheppard, J. T., 51-2
Skinner, B. F., 74
Smiles, Samuel, 132
snobbery of science, 53-6, 106
social class, 70-71
social psychology, 100, 166
social responsibilities of males and females, 87
sociology, 76n, 122, 152
soft and hard, 73, 79, 83-92
Solinus, Julius, 20
Spearman, C., 124
Sprat, Thomas, 104
status, 53-6
Storr, Anthony, 66
Strachey, Lytton, 49
student–teacher relationship: see teaching and teaching methods
subjectivity of judgment, 163
sublimation, 91
Summerfield, A., 112n
symbolism of the body, 71-2

teaching and teaching methods, 11; authoritative knowledge, 122, 128; indoctrination, 93-110; presuppositions, 43
Thematic Apperception Test, 57-8
Thomson, Godfrey, 131-2
Thurstone, L. L., 124
Time, 62
Times, The, 59, 60
Towards the End of the Morning (Frayn), 139-44, 147-9
transactional research, 166

tribal ecology, 137-8
Treisman, A. M., 58
triviality in psychology, 74
Turner's Syndrome, 115-25

university teaching: *see* teaching and
teaching methods
'uses of objects' tests, 83-4
Unicorn myth, 18-28, 57, 71-2, 172,
177

Values, 169-70
Vernon, P. E., 112
Virgin and Son, 23
virility, 88-9
Vizinczey, Stephen, 173

von Neumann, Johnny, 101

Wallach, M. A., 108n
Warneford Hospital, 58
Watson, J. B., 100
Waugh, Evelyn, 48
Whitehead, A. N., 91
Whiting, John, 16
Who's Who study of academics, 65-70,
87
Wittgenstein, Ludwig, 38, 76

Young, Wayland, 89

Zangwill, Oliver, 46, 59, 74, 99-100, 111
Zola, Émile, 157